W9-BGS-362

The Fall of Sukarno

Tarzie Vittachi

THE FALL OF SUKARNO

FREDERICK A. PRAEGER, *Publishers*
New York • Washington

BOOKS THAT MATTER

Published in the United States of America in 1967
by Frederick A. Praeger, Inc., Publishers
111 Fourth Avenue, New York, N.Y. 10003

Published by arrangement with Andre Deutsch Ltd., London, England

Library of Congress Catalog Card Number: 67-20838

Printed in the United States of America

CONTENTS

ACKNOWLEDGMENTS

I am grateful to: my family, for allowing me to give to the preparation of this book time that was properly theirs; to many friends in Indonesia who tolerated my incessant questions and shared their knowledge and understanding with me, even when they were in danger; to Diana Athill, for helping me to see straight; and to Coral Knight, for the labour of typing the manuscript.

T. V.

INTRODUCTION

In Indonesia, during the past 18 months, a drama of epic dimensions has taken place. Yet, partly because the world has been preoccupied with the war in Vietnam, and partly because foreign correspondents were kept away from the scene, disproportionately scant international attention has been given to these events.

What happened in Indonesia has all the ingredients of classical tragedy: there is a "hero" with a tragic flaw to cause his downfall; there is massive human conflict; there is rhetoric; there is bloodshed; there are sudden ironic twists of circumstance evoking pity and terror; there is plot and sub-plot; there is a play within the play; there is comic relief; there is the conflict of virtue and vice; there is human purpose and divine intervention; there are good guys and bad guys, recognisable against a backdrop of traditional beliefs and behaviour; and finally, there is the promise of catharsis.

Within twelve months a communist-backed *coup d'état* has been foiled and the leaders of the Partai Communis Indonesia (which claimed three million members) have been executed; half a million people have been slaughtered – in Java alone, in five months, many more were killed than in five years of the Vietnam war; the three-year undeclared war with Malaysia has been concluded; and a monolithic structure of power, built through twenty years of whimsical dictatorship, has been demolished and replaced by constitutional procedures under which democratic elections are obligatory. Indonesia has decided to abandon the notion of transforming the world through a new international organisation to be called UNNEFO – United Nations of the

New Emerging Forces – and there are positive signs, at long last, that the natural bounty of its islands will be put to the service of its 105,000,000 people.

The "hero" of these events has been President Sukarno. What kind of man is he? The opening words of his autobiography are: "The simplest way to describe Sukarno is to say that he is a great lover. He loves his country, he loves his people, he loves women, he loves art and, above all, he loves himself."

This thumb-nail sketch was Louis Fischer's, not Sukarno's own, but he himself has frequently used it without the formality of quotation marks, and he evidently likes it as an image of himself. He would probably choose to be remembered as a man of power relieved by humanity, and with an engaging gift for candour. The humble epitaph which he has already chosen for himself, with great pride, is: Here lies Bung Karno, the mouthpiece of the Indonesian people.

Like Macbeth, Sukarno enters the scene in a shower of titles: Honourable Doctor Ingénieur, Hadji Raden Sukarno, Commander-in-Chief of the Armed Forces, Chairman of the Supreme Advisory Council, Chief War Administrator, Highest Leader of the National Front, Commander of State Police, Supreme Leader of the All-Indonesia Clergy, first President of the Republic of Indonesia, Prime Minister, Great Leader of the Indonesian Revolution, Sole Interpreter of the Revolution, Mandatory of the People's Provisional Congress, Repository of the Sufferings of the People, and so on and so on.

And, like Macbeth, he has lost these honours in a swift sequence of events starting with murder and moving through prophetic foreboding and catastrophe to self-destruction.

Whatever else he has been or may have been, Sukarno has certainly earned the title Supreme Demagogue of the post-war world. Without a trace of embarrassment he has written: "A shiver went through me when I first discovered I embodied a kind of power that could move the masses."

And again: "To intoxicate the masses until they were heady with the wine of inspiration was all I lived for." And again: "I am a man of the people. I must see them, listen to them, rub against them. I'm happiest when I'm among them. They are the bread of life for me. I feed off the masses."

He could make words sound as though they were the things they stood for. He draped the *padang* with festoons of phrases so that the crowds who came to hear him *believed* that an Indonesia careening down into economic chaos could transform the world. He could make people believe that the mineral wealth of their country was already bulking so heavily in their pockets that they could afford 15-storey palaces rising out of the filth of Djakarta's slums. He could soothe the people, coax them, scold them, and – most effective of all – excite them into accepting his verbal flatulence as a substitute for the goods they needed to make their lives tolerable.

Has he, then, been nothing but a windbag? Has he done nothing for the people who called him *Bung* (brother) and *Bapak* (father)? Far from it. A reporter once asked him what he had given his country except poverty, disease and corruption, and he answered angrily: "I'll tell you what I have done for my country. I have transformed our islands into one nation. This archipelago was inhabited by Javanese, Sumatrans, Sulawesis, Sundanese and so on; Muslims, Christians, Hindus, animists – different cultures, traditions, languages, religious beliefs. Now they are all Indonesians. Is that not an achievement?" And this is true, as even his bitterest detractors must concede. More than a hundred million people who, twenty years ago, thought parochially, now think and feel as one nation.

It is because of Sukarno that Indonesia has escaped the terrors of linguistic centrifugalism which creates such havoc in India. He ordained that Bahasa Indonesia, not (as might have been expected) his own Javanese language, should be adopted as the national language. It is a simple language used by a tiny minority, not loaded with passionate rivalries – and now the people from Sabang to Merauke can talk to one another in a common tongue and write to each other in the common *Rumi* (Roman) script. Sukarno has used language as a means of bringing people together rather than as a weapon for dividing them.

And he has done more. He has given a people long accustomed to creeping about hat in hand a necessary sense of pride. He has said: "Indonesians must overcome self-consciousness and inferiority. Our people need confidence. This I must give them before I am taken away." And although his strutting on the world stage has been one of the main things preventing him from developing the natural resources so abundant at home, even his enemies must allow that they were a tonic to the Indonesians' pride.

Unfortunately, as Sukarno intoxicated the masses, so he intoxicated himself. He fed off the masses and fattened his ego to such gargantuan proportions that he could no longer see beyond the rim of his own self. His autobiography abounds in scathing comments on the comrades who fought beside him during the Revolution: "Hatta and Sjahrir never created any might. All they did was talk" – Hatta was "too dry a man to work magic over the masses" – Sjahrir was "a malcontent" and a "plotter". Sukarno himself was God-guided: "All my life there's been a Supreme Power guarding, guiding and protecting me . . . I am doing God's work. This is what I was born to do."

He became incapable of giving his attention to the realities of nation-building. He sketched the outlines of policy in broad sweeps and was indifferent when no one troubled to fill in the details: "I never thought of mundane things like money. Only people who have never breathed the fire of nationalism can concern themselves with such trivia . . ." When his impoverished people came out on the streets to protest, in spite of suppressive laws, against unprecedented inflation, he could only advise the Indonesian

Economists' Association "not only to tear to pieces books by Engelbrecht, John Maynard Keynes and the like, but throw them in the sea." At about the same time he inaugurated an Outer Space Health Institute in Djakarta to "examine the health of future Indonesian astronauts."

For twenty years Sukarno was able to fly high and fast, propelled by the force of his own verbosity. Now he has been brought down to earth by an opponent he never expected: the students of Djakarta. They, as the following account will show, are the real heroes on the Indonesian story.

T.V.

London, August 1966

Chapter I

POLITICAL MUSICAL CHAIRS

DJAKARTA, April 1965: the walls are black with tar-brush slogans. DOWN WITH NEOCOLONIALISM – LONG LIVE SUKARNO – LONG LIVE NASAKOM – JOINT CHIEFS OF STAFF ARE COUNTER-REVOLUTIONARIES – LONG LIVE THE COMMUNIST PARTY OF INDONESIA – LONG LIVE NASAKOM – HANG THE IMPERIALISTS AND THEIR INDONESIAN STOOGES – DOWN WITH FOREIGN BASES – LONG LIVE NASAKOM – CRUSH MALAYSIA – BAN AMERICAN MOVIES – LONG LIVE NASAKOM – BAN THE BEATLES – LONG LIVE NASAKOM – BAN THE BPS – LONG LIVE NASAKOM – LONG LIVE NASAKOM.

NASAKOM seemed to be in trouble, considering the number of people who were wishing it long life. And so it was.

NASAKOM was President Sukarno's concept of a truly representative government, *NAS* representing the Nationalist Party, *A* standing for Agama, the religious parties, and *KOM* for the Communist Party. Sukarno has always had a gift for telescoped all-inclusive slogans, and this one, which he had decreed as policy, was particularly tightly packed. His cabinet, embracing the three major elements of Indonesian life, was expected to provide the stable government needed to carry the Indonesian Revolution through to its next phase: prosperity at home and a powerful and influential place for Indonesia in the councils of the world. To quote President Sukarno, NASAKOM was "not merely a joining of forces of parties, the party based on nationalism, the party based on religion, and the party based on communism, but it refers to the trends in living society, a new social force or a new revolutionary force that has never existed before in the history of mankind." As he once told a meeting of journalists: "For our part, we are not conducting this struggle to build the world anew with nuclear arms or other instruments of destruction. Our fundamental strength lies in our concepts and ideas."

Unfortunately, theory and practice had proved to be divergent. The NASAKOM cabinet was not the repository of power but merely an instrument of power wielded by the President. The Presidency had been transformed through the years from the office of a chief executive and Head of State responsive and responsible to the people, into a monolithic structure as inaccessible and irreducible as Stalin's. Shaped by the character of the man who occupied it, it had also become wayward and wilful.

Sukarno was no more a communist than Jawaharlal Nehru. He was no less religious than Ayub Khan or Harold Wilson or any other leader of a country whose tradition and constitution provide a place for an officially recognised religion. And if he was more nationalist than most it was because the struggle for his country's independence had been more bitter than most. In theory, therefore, he was in a position to balance the ingredients of NASAKOM, but in fact he treated his own conception with contempt. He deliberately packed the cabinet with men who, by conviction or by calculation, leaned heavily toward the policies of the PKI – the Partai Kommunis Indonesia.

This was read by the world as evidence that Sukarno was himself a communist, or else a pawn of the PKI. But although there was more communism in the cabinet than religion or nationalism, he was neither. Sukarno's political philosophy had always been socialist, extreme from the point of view of those who adhere to the sanctity of private property, private enterprise and the profit motive (had Aneurin Bevan been an Indonesian he would have been a Sukarnoist – or President). But Sukarno's monumental ego never permitted him to accept the discipline of thought and conduct implied by membership of a communist party or by the acceptance of a political line set in Peking or Moscow, or in the Politbureau of the Indonesian Communist Party. For the same reason he had never been, knowingly, the pawn of the PKI, nor of any other organisation. There were simpler and more compelling reasons for his packing the cabinet with a preponderance of communists and crypto-communists.

The communists and the Army were the two most active and powerful organised forces in Indonesia. The Indonesian Armed Forces – the second largest military establishment in Asia – was the only truly disciplined organisation in the country, and President Sukarno, its Commander in Chief, never lacked confidence that it would be obedient to his will. He knew by experience how to manipulate the men within it almost without raising a whimper of protest, as he had done in 1963 when he removed General Nasution (whose righteousness and thorny integrity had always irritated him) by the simple device of "kicking him upstairs". He made him Minister of Defence and put General Yani in as Army Commander; and although Nasution brooded for a while, he ended by trying to make the best of his new job.

So Sukarno was sure of his hold on the Army, and had to find ways and means of bringing Indonesia's second major force, the PKI, to heel. He thought he had the answer. "I have learned", he once said to a confidant, "that the most effective way to earn the respect of the Americans is to abuse them. The only way to win the communists over is to lead them. I have brought them nearer to me so that I can lead them in the way I wish to move." Having given religion, too, a place at the top – if only nominally – he expected no objection from the poorly organised Muslim parties, and should the communists prove restless under his leadership he could always turn the Army on them as he had done in December 1948, in Madiun, when the Army tore apart the communist rebellion led by Amir Sjarifuddin.

An important function of NASAKOM, therefore, was to enable Sukarno to lead the communists along the way he wished to go. But the Communist Party leadership had other routes in mind. That is why NASAKOM was doomed from the start. It provided the communists with the most strategic position they had ever achieved in their forty-five-year history as a formal party in Indonesia.

It gave them respectability in the eyes of the middle class and of officialdom. Being part of the government – in however minor a role – is one of the surest passports to social acceptability in Indonesia, particularly in inbred Java. Party cadres, right down to those in the remotest villages of Makassar, could now speak with some authority and presence. The reputation they had once had of being political bandits was removed. In addition to this, the communists' presence in the cabinet allayed much of the suspicion of the nationalists, who had hitherto looked on the PKI as the party of a foreign power. It convinced many people that Indonesian communists were different from other kinds: they must be, since their leaders, D. N. Aidit, Njoto and M. H. Lukman, had sworn allegiance to the five basic principles of the Republic, and the first of these was belief in One God, and that Muhammad was His Prophet. If Indonesian communists spoke the *sjahadat* – the prayer which affirms that a man is a Muslim – how could they be the infidels which communists elsewhere appeared to be?

There were, of course, many who described this purely formal piety as opportunism and hypocrisy, but they were people who would have abused the PKI anyway. Among the *santris*, the people – particularly the rural people – whose lives were centred on Islam, there was even some display of anger over the PKI's cynicism in publicly proclaiming their faith while their party officials in the villages often and vociferously declared that belief in God and all the practices of religion were vestigial remains of what the Great Leader of the Revolution, Sukarno, had pithily dubbed "the Oldefos" (the Old Established Forces). But still, the fact that Bung Karno himself (*Bung* means brother – the more familiar prefix, *Su*, means The Good) had brought the PKI into the cabinet made it seem possible to the majority that the Great Leader had indeed transformed the communists into Islamic nationalists.

The sense of power which their status in NASAKOM gave them often made the PKI cadres in the more remote outposts act high-handedly towards the peasants. Many instances of forcible expropriation of farmland or paddy fields by the local communist party officials were reported to the *vidanes*. But these village headmen and police officers were often too intimidated to take any action. Higher officials at the district level rarely acted against such expropriations because they could not be sure how Jakarta would react. When Dutch and British owned property was forcibly seized by the PKI, President Sukarno congratulated the "heroes of the Newly Emerging Forces who had taught the reactionaries a deserving lesson." And since the peasants who had been robbed had, in fact, been landowners, however petty, it was not always safe to try to restore their property. This blind-eye treatment caused more and more people to seek redress from the Army commanders of the area. Gradually, the Army came to be regarded by the villagers as the only effective constabulary. Throughout 1965, from Madiun, Solo and other communist strongholds, came increasingly numerous reports of expropriations of paddy fields, and vegetable and cassava plots, and of Army intervention – sometimes leading to bloody clashes with units of communist "volunteers."

One of the more obvious signs of the rapidly increasing

effectiveness of the PKI under NASAKOM was that their scribblers had a virtual monopoly of wall-space for their slogans. At the end of 1964, some of the more moderate elements in the higher political echelons – one of them was Dr Chairul Saleh, Third Deputy Prime Minister – decided that the PKI should not have it all their own way. They decided to form a new political party which, comically but cannily, was called The Body for the Promotion of Sukarnoism. The Bung gave it his blessing to begin with. In fact, when the Communist Aidit demanded at a Cabinet meeting in January 1965 that "this counter-revolutionary BPS should be banned forthwith since its aims were anti-communist", Sukarno reminded him sharply: "I do not like *demands* being made of me. If I ban the BPS I should have to ban *all* political parties." The threat shut Aidit up for the moment and that night the President, in a tone of triumphant self-satisfaction, told a senior member of the Supreme Advisory Council that he had "twisted Aidit's tail till it hurt". But the next morning people in Jakarta, Bandung and Bogor woke up to see that thousands of graffiti experts had been at work. Every inch of wall-space was covered with anti-BPS slogans: GANJANG (chew or crush) BPS – GANTUNG (hang) BPS – BPS-CONTRA-REVOLUSI – HIDUP (long live) NASAKOM – HIDUP NASAKOM. On the second day the road surfaces were chalk-marked with the same slogans. A day later cloth streamers and *pandal* banners were strung across the streets: BUBARKAN (ban) BPS – HIDUP NASAKOM – HIDUP PKI – HIDUP NASAKOM – BUBARKAN BPS – HIDUP NASAKOM. Before the week was out, the President had issued a decree banning the BPS on the ground that it was "a counter-revolutionary distraction" for people engaged in the serious and sacred business of getting on with their Revolution.

As early as 1960 Sukarno had found that whenever he

needed to produce mass feeling against the victim of the moment – the American or British Embassy or, later, the Indian Embassy and the offices of Air India – he only had to tell Aidit. Within four hours the PKI could put on an impressive street demonstration marshalling two to three thousand heroic Davids gaily slinging stones with impunity at foreign Goliaths. Such back-stage cooperation between the President and the PKI increased in intensity as Indonesia's problems at home and abroad became more and more serious.

One of the strangest instances of the closeness of this relationship was that the PKI – to save Sukarno embarrassment – agreed not to organise any communist demonstrations against the soaring prices of household necessities. The price of a kilo of rice was almost as much as an artisan's daily wage. Housing was in wretchedly short supply. The prices of vegetables, fruits and even *kretek* – the clove cigarette smoked by most Indonesians – had trebled between 1963 and 1965. But until 1965, when Aidit judged it was time to begin putting on pressure, there were no PKI-sponsored public demands for the lowering of prices. And Aidit went even further in his cooperative attitude: he promised to discourage other demonstrators from bringing the NASAKOM Government into disrepute by demanding the impossible. As events later showed, Aidit had different ideas about how and when to attack Sukarno. For the present, Sukarno was the best bulwark the PKI had against the Army, the hostility of which was becoming more and more apparent. The PKI needed Sukarno as much as Sukarno needed them to maintain a kind of tentative order in the poverty-stricken cities.

This mutual dependence increased Aidit's stature with President Sukarno. Aidit was careful not to show by anything he said or did that he was growing more effectively powerful among the workers and peasants than the aging Sukarno, who had become increasingly sybaritic at home and increasingly concerned with his image abroad

When he was slapped down by Sukarno for "*demanding*" the banning of the BPS, Aidit – outside the Cabinet room – asked *Bapak* (father) for his forgiveness. The President later related this incident to members of his Supreme Advisory Council, at least one of whom was more impressed by the fact that the President had sounded childishly pleased that the tough little Aidit had apologised than they were by Aidit's motives or behaviour. It was indeed a revealing incident. Aidit had begun to flex his muscles and realise how strong his position had become as a result of his membership of the Cabinet and the President's increasing political dependence on him.

In early 1965 he made another "demand" – this time in public: that the President should decree the arming of "15,000,000 workers and peasants to wage the war against the so-called Malaysia." Arms, he said, would be forthcoming from Peking. President Sukarno, an old fox at scenting out motivations, knew immediately that Malaysia had nothing to do with Aidit's demand, and it was curtly refused.

Aidit needed an army for his own reasons: to meet the challenge of General Yani and the Indonesian Army who, as soon as he made an open bid for power, would move once again to crush the PKI as they had done before, following the Madiun uprising. Aidit had no intention of being executed by an army firing squad as Armi Sjarifuddin had been in 1948. The situation was very different in the Indonesia of 1965 and would probably be even more different soon. In 1948 Sjarifuddin had tried to take power in a country whose people were still buoyantly proud of their success in wresting their independence away from an imperialist power; a country whose acknowledged leader was at the height of his patriotic zeal and physical and mental powers. In 1965 Aidit was planning to make a bid for power in a country which had suffered economic privation for more than twenty years; whose people were living on a diet of grand illusions and slogans provided by Sukarno; and – more significant – a country whose Greater Leader and Sole Interpreter of the Revolution was expected to die at any moment.

For two years the air had been thick with rumours about the President's ill health. By the beginning of 1964 his death was reported by the bazaar gossips to be imminent. The fact that he was being attended by a team of Chinese doctors, among them acupuncturists, gave substance to these stories and created the impression that his illness was "incurable" by ordinary medicine and, therefore, grave. Indonesian doctors at the Djakarta General Hospital diagnosed, on the basis of these rumours, advancing kidney failure. One of these doctors who had attended the President said that he would "probably not be able to enjoy the Lebaran feast this year [December 1965] unless he submitted to surgery." Sukarno would not do that because – again according to popular belief – there was an astrological prediction that he would "die under the knife". Sukarno, however, confounded the fears of his friends and the wishful thinking of his enemies by living on lustily and enjoying not only the *selamatans* (feasts) of Lebaran but also pleasures of a more virile and strenuous kind. The same physician said that the President had been advised in 1964 that he would have to go easier on his sexual acrobatics in the future. The President had asked, "If I stay away from women how long can I live?" "Two years, Bapak," the doctor had replied with grim deference. The President laughed with his reply: "Why should I bother then to prolong my life if I must stay away from women?"

These rumours of Sukarno's impending death, whatever their basis, provide one of the vital clues to an understanding of the political events within Indonesia for a period of over two years. They were to play a significant part in the events of September 30, 1965, which caused the crackdown on the

PKI and the real beginning of the President's downfall. The strategy of every political party and faction was to be there, next to the Bung's chair, when the music stopped. Efforts made in 1965 by Dr Sumitro, once Indonesia's Finance Minister and a fugitive from the Bung's wrath for many years, to organise Indonesians abroad into a legion of exiles, failed disastrously for this very reason: no one thought it was the right time to oppose the Bung. With the end so near, this was the time to seem to support him and get near the centre of power, as Aidit and the PKI had already done. This, too, was the motivation behind the formation of the Body for the Promotion of Sukarnoism – it was not Sukarno or Sukarnoism that were being promoted, but the political fortunes of the architects of the BPS, Chairul Saleh and other members of the banned Partai Murbak, the "Trotskyite" socialists.

Chapter II

TO HELL WITH THE WORLD

The PKI gave Sukarno continuous and vociferous support in the campaign against Malaysia, so much so that it is difficult to say whether the idea of *konfrontasi* was Sukarno's own or had come from the PKI. What is plain is that it suited the PKI admirably, since crushing Malaysia was an essential part of the Asian aims of Peking.

Lacking the means to win the confidence of the people by public service, every political group was compelled to resort to propaganda. But, as each party grew, it was banned by President Sukarno because according to his political philosophy there was room for only one party in Indonesia – the party of the Revolution. He allowed for shades of opinion within this broad category but he took to himself the sole right to decide when a party overstepped the limits and thus became *kontra-revolusi*, *reaksi* and dangerous to the Republic. Once banned, no party had been known to reappear. Out of the plethora of political parties engendered by the Revolution only eight remained intact in 1965: the Partai Nasionalis Indonesia – founded by Sukarno himself; the Partai Kommunis Indonesia, founded in 1920 and led till his death in 1965 by Dipa Nusantara Aidit; the Beparki (the party of the Chinese community); the Nahdatul Ulama (the party of the Religious Scholars); the Partai Kristen Indonesia (the Protestants' Party); the Partai Katolik (the Catholic party); the PSII (the party of the Muslim Political Associations); and Partindo (Partai Indonesia). As each party went under, its newspapers and broadsheets were banned.

Sukarno had his own ideas about the function of the press: "I hope that the Asian-African press will become an instrument of the Revolution of Mankind that is transforming the world, that is destroying the old order built on domination and oppression, that is building the world anew, ensuring true national independence, social justice and abiding peace." (Afro-Asian Journalists' Conference, 1963.) It was not a bad definition – not very different from the way that Walter Lippman or James Reston or Baron Williams or any of the major stalwarts of the Western Press would have described the role of the press – but the catch was that the Indonesian press was expected to identify national interest with that of the President and his henchmen even when they were corrupt or incompetent. Mochtar Lubis, the Editor of the *Indonesia Raya*, was arbitrarily punished by Dr Sukarno for the crime of having campaigned for a cleaner administration. Lubis, who had fought as hard as anyone else for Indonesian independence, watched with growing horror how the cancer of corruption was sapping the vitality of the new country and asked: "Was it for this that we became free?" He was sent to prison in 1956 and his newspaper was made forfeit to the State. All appeals from his colleagues at home and abroad that he should at least be brought to trial and charged with whatever offences he was alleged to have committed were of no avail. He was a personal prisoner of the President. It took a change of government nine years later before he was freed.

The Partai Socialist Indonesia, once led by Dr Sultan Sjahrir who had been Prime Minister of three successive governments in the years immediately following on the Revolution of 1945, was banned in 1962 and he and some of his colleagues were imprisoned on allegations (not charges) of having plotted to assassinate President Sukarno and take over the country. Rosihan Anwar, the distinguished editor of the Socialist newspaper *Pedoman*, at that time the best managed and widest circulating newspaper in Java

(70,000), was threatened with closure if he did not sign a nineteen point document of "undertakings" imposed on the Indonesian press that year. Anwar signed the document, although he realised that it was against his ideals of free journalism, because he was certain that the situation would soon take a turn for the better. He believed that he should continue to publish under the charter, against the day when the lights went on again. After he signed, *Pedoman* was confiscated anyway by direct order of the President.

The form of confiscation of newspapers devised by Sukarno was unique in its iniquitousness. He confiscated the assets of a newspaper and not its liabilities. The expropriated owner was therefore still under obligation to reimburse his creditors – the suppliers of machinery, newsprint and inks – without the collateral on which credit had been established or the means to make repayments. A year after the banning of *Pedoman* I walked up the driveway to Anwar's bungalow and found him sitting in a wicker chair in his verandah gazing fixedly at the trees outside. He was startled to see me again after two years. He smiled a little sheepishly when I asked him how he had been occupying himself since *Pedoman* had been killed. "Sitting here," he said ruefully. "What else is there to do but wait?" I asked what he had been staring at so intently. "That truck," he said, pointing to a fairly new vehicle standing under the coconut palms. "That truck is all I saved from the plunder. I was thinking how much I could sell it for now. Maybe 15 million? 20 million? But it is secondhand. Maybe only 7 million? My family can live on that for some time. Things may change, who knows?"

With such a strict control over the press, it was not difficult for the government to convince the public that they were in imminent danger of being overrun by Malaysia. Street posters showed how Tengku Abdul Rahman, the Malaysian Prime Minister, with a look of bestial ferocity, was pointing a kris at the heart of Indonesia. Visiting

Indonesia the day after the Malaysian General Election of 1964, in which the Tengku's Alliance Party had won 85 per cent of the seats in Parliament, I was appalled by the gullibility of even highly educated Indonesians who had believed the story in their newspapers that British soldiers, with bayonets fixed, had stood watch at every polling booth in Malaysia to see that the voters marked their ballots in favour of the Tengku. When I told them that I had been there myself and had gone round the polling booths to see how the elections were going but had not seen a single British soldier about, with or without bayonets, they became doubtful – but only about my sanity. When I said that if the British wanted to rig an election they had enough experience and intelligence to set about it more discreetly, they gave me that quaintly sympathetic look which they reserved for the out and out *nekolim* (neocolonialist).

People who did not read newspapers got their propaganda through radio, television and the wall scribblings. Each morning the headlines of the day were there on the walls. By the end of 1964 Djakarta was momentarily expecting a Malaysian invasion through Medan in North Sumatra, and bombing raids on the capital. For months the news media had built up this "*nekolim-phobie*". Radio Djakarta had told people night in, night out, about the need to prepare for a stab in the back by that "arch-villain, Tengku Abdul Rahman", aided, of course, by the British Imperialists. But there was hope offered also. Indonesia was now able to make her own "bom". An Indonesian physicist had found the formula for making an atom bomb, working from scratch. All his own work, as the commentator announced. No obligations to Rutherford, Fermi, Oppenheim or any of those *nekolims*. So Indonesia would soon become a nuclear power, and any doubts as to whether she should make an atom bomb before making a bicycle were frowned upon as typical *nekolim* cynicism.

The hysteria became more intense when President

Sukarno, with dramatic suddenness, withdrew Indonesia from the UN. This impulsive decision horrified even his friend and straightman Dr Subandrio who, as Foreign Minister, had to carry out the order. He delayed the formal letter of withdrawal for three weeks before he signed it, hoping that the Bung would change his mind. But so much public fuss had been made of it that even had he wished to recant, Sukarno did not have the face to take the step, especially since Tengku Abdul Rahman had publicly chortled: "Good riddance." Dr Subandrio told his officials that the decision had been "too whimsical". It had been provoked by the admission of Malaysia to one of the temporary, rotating vacancies on the Security Council. Subandrio had been planning to make a major personal impact on the UN at the 1965 session by an international campaign, climaxed by the "Second Bandung" Asian-African meeting scheduled to take place in Algeria in the summer. The President's decision had shot his hopes down in flames.

The PKI was jubilant. Its mentors in Peking cheered solemnly, and encored when Sukarno began to rough out publicly a new concept of "Anti-colonial United Nations" – the United Nations of the New Emerging Forces – to which, he believed, the neutralist countries of Africa and Asia would flock, abandoning the UN in New York as he had done. The general exodus, he expected, would turn the United Nations building in New York into a gravestone to the hopes of the New Emerging Forces that had once resided there.

This was not the first time that President Sukarno had decided to resign from the world. He had already organised GANEFO, the Games of the New Emerging Forces, as a counter-attraction to the Olympic Games which, in his opinion, were controlled by reactionaries who admitted countries without political or moral validity, such as Israel, Taiwan and Malaysia. Leaving the UN was just another inevitable step for a man who said publicly, over and over again, that his motto and that of Indonesia was "live dangerously". He told the Ceylon Ambassador soon after making his decision to leave the UN that "living dangerously", doing something entirely unexpected, something that shocked the rest of the world, gave him a "sense of the eagle". The thrill of that stratospheric loneliness and the knowledge of the impact that the power he wielded could have on other beings must have been irresistible to a man to whom megalomania had become a habit.

"For me myself – besides thanking God Almighty – it has strengthened my conviction that it may be a justification of God Almighty that the basis of my leadership to the Indonesian Nation, that everything I have given to the Indonesian Nation, every 'ism' I have given to the Indonesian people, the way in which to unite the Indonesian people, the way how others with me mobilised the Indonesian people, the way of implanting self-help in the Indonesian people, in short all the policy I have given to the Indonesian Nation, has got the approval of God Almighty because God Almighty has for five times given me His protection."*

In 1963 Sukarno issued a new map of the world. In this the Indian Ocean was renamed the Indonesian Ocean and zero meridian was transferred from Greenwich to Djakarta.

Leaving the United Nations brought Sukarno much nearer to Peking and its Indonesian ally, the PKI. His stature, barely acknowledged by Chou en Lai at the Bandung Conference in 1955, was now generously conceded by the great Mao himself. But even eagles must eat. Indonesia desperately needed foreign assistance to import foodstuffs, clothing and essential household articles. The United States and the West had been told to "go to Hell" with their aid. Quitting the UN also meant losing the assistance of the UN's agencies such as the Food and

*Five attempts had been made to assassinate President Sukarno.

Agricultural Organisation and the World Health Organisation, which had done good work in Indonesia. Indonesia had enormous debts, mostly accumulated under bilateral credit agreements, for the supply of arms, building materials and consumer goods. By July 1965 the foreign debt had grown to over two billion dollars. Nearly seventy per cent of this was owed to the USSR which, unprepared to write it off as a contribution to New Emerging Forces, was demanding repayment of matured credits.

As far back as May 1962 Sukarno had formulated his public attitude towards international cooperation. During an address at the celebration of National Reawakening Day he said: "Look, many countries in Asia are in fact not standing on their own power, are not relying on their own force. These countries may look prosperous but live on help, live on aid, live on money poured on them by another country. When those countries lose these supports they will collapse. The Indonesian Nation does not want to become such a country, my brothers . . . to rely on one's own strength, to rely on one's own power, to rely on one's own capability, to foster, to build, to bundle together one's forces. No mendicancy. Self-reliance. No mendicancy."

But rhetoric which warms the heart does not fill the rice pot, and in fact international mendicancy became as much a part of Indonesia's life as it was of India's. Foreign exchange or credit was needed to buy food for Indonesia's fast-growing population of 105,000,000 whose needs could no longer be met from home-grown rice. The villagers, accustomed to a subsistence livelihood, eked out an existence on their miniscule garden plots, and did not feel the weight of the nation's predicament except when there was a natural disaster such as they had experienced in 1963 when the rats ate up the paddy crop in East and Central Java. Then they had been reduced to scooping out the soft core of the trunks of banana trees and boiling it for the day's meal. Some of them had been infuriated by the widely publicised remark attributed to the President: "let them eat the rats", but very soon they had been able to revert to their normal lives. The earth in Java is bountiful. It was feeding the townspeople which was the problem. Each year, the gap between home production of rice and the total needed was increasing. By 1965 it had grown to forty per cent. The food import bill was growing accordingly and it had to be paid for in foreign money. Foreign money was also needed for importing spare parts to maintain public utilities. For fifteen years very little maintenance had been done. By 1965 "the spare parts drought" as a Djakarta economist called it, had become critical. The railways were becoming derelict, public transport was grossly inadequate and fares were rising steeply. A journey from Djakarta to Malan in East Java, or even to nearer Bandung, had become a major undertaking unless one could afford to hire a car or to fly. It cost a Djakarta woman more than her quarterly income to buy a train ticket to visit her husband who was a political prisoner in Madiun jail, 800 kilometres away.

The telecommunications system was T-model and needed replacing. The cars, *bemos* and *betjaks* that choked the city streets, took a daily pounding from the pothole-pitted roads and were in constant need of repair. But turners and mechanics were rare and, even when available, were unable to make up the parts for want of tools.

The massive military establishment was equipped with the most modern tanks and weapons. Russian and American tanks bustled about on practice manoeuvres. Russian-built MIGs zoomed across the skies above the air bases at Halim and Madiun. They needed heavy maintenance. The Russians, who had once thought that they would do good business by supplying military equipment cheap to Indonesia and making their profits out of the supply of spares, were now refusing to supply any unless they were recompensed according to the agreed repayment schedule.

Foreign exchange was essential to carry out the President's

prestige building programme. Each time he held an international event, a new complex of modern buildings went up in Djakarta, rising with superb disdain from the mud and slums around it. The Hotel Indonesia, the Asian Games *kompleks*, and the new sky-scrapers intended for a Conference of New Emerging Forces, were all Sukarno's dreams of what modern Indonesia should look like. This anxiety to play it big was reflected also in the sumptuousness of the Indonesian embassies abroad. It mattered little to Sukarno that it was all a hollow facade which never fooled anyone.

All this extravagance was possible only at the sacrifice of the Indonesian economy which was being held up by the foreign props which the President so eloquently denounced. Despite the grand gesture of renouncing mendicancy as a way of living, Indonesia – having turned its face away from the rest of the world – was compelled to ask for aid from Peking – to beg for more aid. Arms for the love of Allah, was the new prayer. They were offered generous credit terms for military equipment, engineering tools, and heavy machinery, and a grant of seventy-five per cent of the estimated cost of the buildings to house CONEFO – the conference of New Emerging Forces. This new *kompleks* was to be the headquarters of UNNEFO, the new United Nations that Sukarno was planning to establish for the Third World. The foreign debt mounted monstrously as the repayment schedules were neglected. Indonesia's financial credit abroad fell disastrously. At one stage Dr Subandrio, with the connivance of General Omar Dani, commander of the Indonesian Air Force, thought up a quick way to make some foreign exchange and, at the same time, requite a part of their obligation to Peking. When Russia stopped China's supplies, following the Sino-Soviet rift, spare parts for the MIGs Indonesia had received from Russia were sold to Peking. Airforce officers have even alleged that Indonesian MIGs in use were cannibalised for this purpose.

But, however short of foreign exchange the country was,

President Sukarno remained bent on playing the international grandee. He offered $4,000,000 to Prince Sihanouk of Cambodia as Indonesia's contribution toward the expenses of the second Games of the New Emerging Forces to be held in Pnom Penh. He was fond of declaring in public: "I am no economist", in tones which seemed to suggest that economics was for book-keepers, and a concern for economic development was a certain symptom of anti-nationalism. "Let us transform the world", he told the Asian-African Journalists Conference in 1963. "We must fight the remnants of the old regimes that linger in men's minds. We must fight the attitudes of paternalism, of the inherent superiority of elites, we must fight the conservatism that those regimes engendered. We must fight the dogmatism of pet theories, of fixed ideologies and of narrow creeds. We must fight the intolerance of race and of everything that we ourselves are not." There was no reference to the need to fight against the poverty of the people in this land more blessed with material potential, human buoyancy, natural beauty and spiritual gifts than almost any other country in the world.

Chapter III

THE DOWNWARD SPIRAL

The President's not being an economist would not have mattered so much if his deputy had felt the inclination and had been given the responsibility and authority to attend to the mundane business of making two ears of rice grow where one grew before. But Dr Subandrio, brilliant though his mind was, could not bring himself to pay attention to economic development. As First Deputy to the President he was virtually Prime Minister, a job which made him responsible for the general administration and development of the country. But the elegant "Bandrio", the scintillating conversationalist who could dazzle the most sceptical journalist with his cruel wit and easy charm, did not care to put his brains to the heavy task of working out ways and means by which the natural resources of soil-rich Indonesia could be made to work for the people. To be fair, it must be said that the prospect had appalled men of far higher intellectual calibre, among them Herr Schacht, the financial wizard of Germany, who once took a long look at the Indonesian situation, shook his hoary head sadly and left as soon as he decently could.

Many economic experts came and went. Their reports piled up in the Ministry files unheeded by anyone who mattered. The most recent of these visits was by the celebrated Dutch economist, Jan Tinbergen. As a socialist and a critic of the shortcomings of *laissez-faire* international capitalism, Tinbergen was possibly the adviser best suited to deal with Indonesia's particular problems and the political predilections of its rulers. But he too left Djakarta in profound sadness. He could find no one except *fonction-*

naires to listen to the advice he had come to give. When he was allowed to meet President Sukarno he tried to bring up the subject of his report, but he was fobbed off at every turn. Palace intimates say that the President, sensing at one stage what Tinbergen had in mind, said half indulgently, half seriously, "Professor, if you talk about *mijn gebouwen* (my buildings) I will not listen."

Sukarno's buildings must, indeed, have been on the professor's agenda for his discussion with the President. The prestige building projects in Djakarta, the victory monuments – these were already part of the city's joke-lore. The Pillar of Freedom in Djakarta, designed as a crested torch with a massive gold flame, intended to awe and impress people with the sense of freedom, evoked bazaar remarks about Sukarno's interest in all things phallic. (This comment, it should be made clear, was not intended as an insult, certainly not at the time the monument was erected – when Sukarno was still at the height of his power. Indonesian people, particularly the Javanese, have a profound and persistent sense of symbolism in their daily lives. They make swift connections between event and event, or between person and event, and they draw rich symbolic values from them.)*

The intellectuals joked about these expensive show-pieces and the futility of sumptuous department stores run by the government, when Indonesia was bankrupt; but in the villages, where the vast majority of Indonesians live, there was much less evidence of disenchantment. For people accustomed to a subsistence livelihood, existing at a minimum level of nutrition and physical mobility, the fact that the dollar was exchanging at 10,000 rupial or 60,000-rupiah

*The *wayang* plays, the puppet drama of Indonesia, probably arose out of this addiction to symbols. The characters in the plays and the situations they find themselves in, are frequently identified with living people and current events. Indonesians will ask: what interest would there now be in these ancient dramas of the battle between good and evil – Arjuna, the high-born, versus the satanic beings – unless their symbols expressed eternal values?

had little or no significance. They were much more concerned with not being able to buy a flashlight battery or a rubber tube for their bicycles, or because the price of *kretek* cigarettes, once the cheapest in the world (and the best, in the opinion of some connoisseurs), was rising abominably high. The rupiah they received from the government for the rice bought for the Army seemed to buy less and less cloth and fringe necessities, such as refined sugar and better quality tea, but most people were inclined to blame this situation not on the extravagance of the government so much as on the villainy of Malaysia and the British, who were threatening to destroy Indonesia. That is what the newspapers and Radio Djakarta said every day. Even the *santris*, the religious-minded people, the remnants of the banned Masjumi and Darul Islam parties and the adherents of the Nahdatul Ulama party (the party of the Muslim religious teachers), who were more concerned with rampant irreligiousness or with the spreading influence of unorthodox spiritual societies than with problems of national economic degradation, shared with the infidel communists their certainty that the troubles of Indonesia were the fault of Malaysia. Malaysia, they all agreed, should be crushed.

Dr Subandrio once declared that the swift economic development in Malaysian Borneo was "an act of aggression against Indonesia" because it was intended to show up the backwardness of Kalimantan – Indonesian Borneo.

This was the basis of the superb confidence that President Sukarno and Dr Subandrio displayed, standing in the ruins of Indonesia's currency structure and foreign trade. Subandrio even had the hide to make a public announcement that anyone who believed or said that "economic development" in Indonesia was more important than "national development" was a misguided *nekolim* agent and a counter-revolutionary. On his instructions Antara, the State News Agency, issued to the newspapers an article explaining the cause of inflation in Indonesia. Under the signature of "A High Official of the Bank Negara" the article explained that "various currencies known as 'United States dollars', 'British Pound Sterling' and 'so-called Malaysian dollars' have been injected into the economy of Indonesia by the agents of Neocolonialism and Imperialism in order to weaken our currency and destroy us." The punishment for such practices was death.

The newspapers and Radio Djakarta put out this kind of alibi as an explanation of the chaotic currency situation. The rural people and large numbers of the semi-literate urban population may have been taken in, but those who dealt in foreign trade knew how to negotiate currency. The blackmarket in foreign exchange was so widespread that it was generally referred to as the "open market". No one – not even, according to rumour, President Sukarno himself – operated at the official rates. Hong Kong was the base for most of these operations and the most adept and trusted dealers were to be found among the Chinese (during the student demonstrations against high prices and corruption in high places, the Ministers who had tame Chinese foreign exchange operators in tow were named).

Every now and then, when imported goods in common use had run out and the currency prices in Pesar Baru were sky-rocketing, the government would resort to quick but very temporary deflationary devices. At such times the Banks would arbitrarily restrict the amount of cash that a single customer could withdraw on any one day. This tended to frighten off the exchange operators and depress the prices they were willing to pay for foreign money; but only for a day or two, till they had rigged up devices for drawing out through cheque payments to nominees who would provide the cash needed indirectly. In June 1965 when the price of a dollar was rising beyond 10,000 – which at that time seemed the point of no return – the government raised the "tourist rate" for the dollar from 350 to 4,500, thus bringing the open market price of the dollar tumbling down to 5,000.

Everybody, overnight, became a tourist. Official exchange rates had become so absurd that the government itself unofficially recognised seven or eight permissible rates. In January 1965, there was 1) the official rate, pegged for many years at 45 rupiahs to one dollar; 2) the "business rate" of 350 rupiah to the dollar; 3) the "tourist rate" of 500 to the dollar; 4) the "American Embassy" rate of 1,000 rupiahs to the dollar, available to all diplomatic missions for their local expenses and staff wages; 5) the "official's rate" (not to be confused with the official rate) of 1,600 to the dollar – available to public servants who had their superior's favour and were thus recommended to the bank; 6) the "Hotel Indonesia rate" of 3,000 rupiah to the dollar – this was also popularly called "the Cabinet rate"; and 7) the "open rate" of 5,000 rupiah to the dollar. Within two months, the Cabinet rate stood at 5,000 and the open rate at 7,500; by June anyone with a dollar could buy 10,000 rupiah.

Not unexpectedly, wages and salaries, calculated many years ago on the basis of simple barter values, did not rise commensurately with the value of the rupiah in terms of foreign currency. The salary of a senior doctor in charge of a hospital of 6,000 patients was 6,000 rupiah a month – 60 cents. How did he manage on this to feed, clothe and educate his six children? "Oh, it's not so bad", he said. "I get an allowance of rice from the government at subsidised prices, I spend nothing on transport since I live near the hospital, and my rent is subsidised." He made up the gap between the daily needs of rice and the government supply with "cassava, sweet potatoes and other yams." To go with the rice there was *sambal* (chillies, onions and salt pounded together), vegetables were cheap in Malan where he lived, and coconut was plentiful. Meat and fish were rare delicacies. The real problem arose when anything manufactured was needed – a fountain pen, a new frame for his spectacles, light bulbs or the simple finery that his wife and children needed to make their lives tolerably varied.

Those who were able to get their hands on some foreign currency were able to make out reasonably well. Pasar Baru in Djakarta, and other bazaars in any of the big towns, were stocked with goods only obtainable if one had access to foreign exchange which could be converted into rupiah at the "open market" rate. Australian canned butter and cheese were available for $1.50, English marmalade at $2.00, a carton of British or American cigarettes at $4.00, and the goods were openly displayed for sale. But they were far beyond the reach of anyone except the visitor who had undeclared foreign currency or travellers cheques, and the few Indonesian businessmen who had foreign contacts.

The one thing that was cheap, ridiculously cheap, was petrol. Until November 1965 a litre of petrol (about half a gallon) was 4.5 rupiah, while a litre of rice was 600 rupiah, and a packet of Indonesian cigarettes was 500 rupiah. The price of this locally refined petrol was pegged by the government and stood at the same level till December 1965 when it was put up by 6,000 per cent.

When credit abroad was curtailed and the spare parts crisis began to hit the few industries which existed, they were compelled to cut back to twenty per cent of their capacity. The export target set for 1965 was $600 million, but only $250 million was available for imports of consumer goods, raw materials and replacements of machinery. The budget deficit for 1965 was estimated at 1,400 billion rupiah – an astronomical sum when one considers that it had to be met from taxes and revenues earned in rupiah, and not in terms of the foreign exchange value of the rupiah. The only plant working at full capacity was the mint – turning out an increasing volume of rupiah notes whose value dropped with each note produced.

President Sukarno and his Cabinet watched the economy plunging downward but could do nothing to put the brake on. There was not even an effort to cut back on State expenditure. When President Sukarno felt he needed a bullet-proof Cadillac it was flown to him by special charter. When he travelled abroad he chartered a plane for himself and his entourage. Entire hotels were reserved for him on his travels, and when foreign correspondents wrote about these extravagances they were banned from entering Indonesia. Sukarno complained bitterly to President Kennedy that *Time* magazine and other American journals treated him with discourtesy. Kennedy sidestepped by saying that he himself received no better treatment from the American Press. (It is strange how men like Sukarno and Sihanouk, who constantly denounce the press as a worthless medium which fools only the gullible, should be so sensitive to its opinions about themselves.) When Sukarno was asked pointedly by a newspaperman (who was never let in again) what he had to strut so proudly about when the economy of his country was in a shambles, he answered: "I'll tell you what I have to be proud about. In twenty years I have made this country of 7,000 islands, from Sabang to Merauke, stretching wider than the United States of America, composed of people of different heritage, speaking different tongues with varying demands and needs, into ONE NATION. They are all Indonesians now. They all speak one language. They think like I do – as an Indonesian. They feel as I do – as Indonesians who will never permit colonialism and imperialism to invade our shores again in whatever form they take. Is that not something to be proud of?" When the reporter persisted that this did not prevent the government from trying to develop the rich potential of Indonesia, Sukarno became furious. "Don't you understand that there is more to this life than becoming rich? People like you can only think of success in terms of material things. Economics is all you ever think of. You think that people, human beings can be bought with money. I'll tell you something. The other day the Americans sent me a few million dollars aid and it was clear that they expected me to show my gratitude by changing my tune about the West. At the same time Krushchev sent me six mangoes, with his love. Which gift do you think I value more? Sukarno cannot be bought for money. He can be bought with love."

Sukarno's boast about welding the scattered archipelago he inherited from the Dutch into a single nation in one generation was not an idle one. This indeed has been his great achievement. The adoption as the national language of Bahasa Indonesia, a "manufactured" language used by a tiny minority of people, made it possible for Indonesia to avoid the terrible peril of linguistic warfare that countries like India, Ceylon and Malaysia continually face. Being a Javanese, with a long and proud cultural heritage, Sukarno could have pandered to the wishes of the vastly preponderant Javanese people and decreed that their language should become the common tongue of the nation. But because he was President of a polyglot country, he felt he should be more than a Javanese, and took the decision which probably saved Indonesia from breaking up many years ago: to make Bahasa Indonesia the national language and to adopt the Roman script. Both these decisions were undeniably "solidarity makers", a phrase which he was fond of using.

But both he and his one-time heir-apparent, Dr Subandrio, made the incredible blunder of convincing themselves that "solidarity making" and economic progress were mutually exclusive undertakings. The distinction that Subandrio made between "economic development" and "national development" was spurious. It was only an alibi for the failure of the Sukarno-Subandrio combination to give Indonesia the thrust needed to achieve its potential as one of the richest countries in the world. They were too preoccupied with transforming the world to bother about their own back garden.

Dr Subandrio told the Council of World Affairs in New Delhi on February 1963: "It is our task and duty to contribute to the right direction of world development in establishing justice, prosperity and peace. We cannot escape from this obligation. This feeling of solidarity of the newly emerging forces is a prerequisite component beside the accumulation of wealth by a few nations if we are determined to keep world development from any kind of domination and hegemony." This kind of rhetoric was the preoccupation of Indonesia's first minister while his country was falling headlong into bankruptcy.

Chapter IV

INDONESIAN HAMLET

It was with ill-concealed suspicion that the Army generals watched the President and his closest political intimate, Dr Subandrio, indulging in their "solidarity making". They obeyed the President as their Commander-in-Chief and respected him as the chief founder of free Indonesia, but, being practical men by training, they wondered about the wisdom of involving themselves in world-building when Indonesia itself was a shambles. And there were other developments which disturbed them even more. They saw how the Air Force and the Marine Corps – the KKO – were falling more and more under the influence of Dr Subandrio. General Omar Dani, head of the Air Force, was known to them as a communist. There were complaints from senior officers that promotions in the Air Force were going to the most voluble advocates of Peking's foreign policy. The Marine Corps had apparently been even more thoroughly infiltrated by men inclined towards Peking.

The Army had played their role with style and courage in the West Irian campaign, and two of its divisions had borne the rigours of the anti-Malaysian campaign on the Borneo-Sarawak border with considerable fortitude. But, as the confrontation dragged on, these troops found themselves being more harrassed by the "volunteers" sent from Djakarta than by the enemy across the fence. These volunteers had been picked by Dr Subandrio and were armed with Chinese weapons brandmarked "*Chung*" (peace). They had been given a rudimentary training in the use of arms but their political indoctrination was profound. At the

Kalimantan (Borneo) Front they were given privileged treatment and better quarters and rations than the regular Army. Frequent quarrels took place between Army men and these volunteers who were inclined, like most amateur soldiers, to strut. The Army resented their tendency to behave like heroes long before they had heard a shot fired in anger or fear. By 1964 the generals began to suspect that Dr Subandrio was building up his own private army which, used in conjunction with the Air Force and the KKO, could be formidable.

Dr Subandrio announced in 1964 that 21,000,000 volunteers had responded to his call for a "national mobilisation to crush Malaysia". As Subandrio rose to pre-eminence under the giant shadow of Sukarno, the distance between the generals and the President widened. Sukarno began to rely increasingly on the "brilliant Bandrio" as he often called him, for his briefing as well as for the comforting he needed in the loneliness of his eagle's eyrie.

Often when he could not sleep because of his chronically defective kidney, he would telephone Subandrio and ask him to come over to the Palace clad in his sarong, just to sit by the presidential bed and talk about the way the world was moving. Sometimes the President would say "Let's talk about anything but politics", but the conversation would inevitably drift towards a dissection of the motivations of the key actors in the tragicomedy going on in Indonesia. Whenever Subandrio sensed that he was pressing things too hard, he would talk about women.

Subandrio, the aesthete, became to Sukarno what Krishna Menon, the ascetic, was to Nehru before the Indian Congress leaders got Menon sacked from the Defence Ministry during the Chinese war with India in 1962. The parallel between the two men seems more and more apt as one studies their relationship with their masters. Consider their political views, their talents as speakers and theoreticians, their inability to get along with anyone except the man they served, their overweening arrogance which came largely from their intellectual contempt for their contemporaries. Subandrio's rise and fall followed much the same course as Menon's. They were their countries ambassadors in London at the same time. They both had a strangely ambivalent love-hate attitude towards Britain. In 1952 Subandrio even recommended from London that Indonesia should apply for "associate membership of the British Commonwealth". This was the man who later belaboured Malaysia for being an "imperialist lackey" because it preferred to remain under the shelter of the Commonwealth rather than trust the protection of Indonesia.

Menon, at one time, wanted to pursue a political career in England. He once represented a ward in the Borough Council of St Pancras. Both Menon and Subandrio took the neutralism which their masters had proclaimed into channels which led their countries into a relationship with China and estranged them from the West. Both fell when the government of their countries turned against Peking. Subandrio in the classical tradition of all grand viziers, used his association with Sukarno to turn his mind against any possible challenger to his privileged position.

General Abdul Haris Nasution was his first target. Sukarno and Nasution disliked each other, feared each other and secretly admired each other. Nasution, a quietly contemplative introvert, a student of the science of war; a liberal democrat, the acme of discretion and cautiousness, a man of prim personal integrity – Indonesia's Hamlet in uniform – was the very opposite of the blustering, rumbustious Sukarno who cut corners, tilted at windmills, changed his friendships as fast as he changed his wives and spat in the world's eye when the world tittered or disapproved. Nasution was meticulous over detail, Sukarno was the painter on broad canvas. Sukarno who respected no one except his own parents (and that only because he felt – and said – that they were blessed in having been his progenitors) was made nervous by Nasution's reserve and deep-rooted sincerity. Subandrio succeeded in turning the President's nervousness into suspicion, and convinced him that Nasution's constancy was in reality his tragic flaw – his refusal "to move with the revolution".

The President understood how to use Nasution's qualities and his reputation without conceding anything to him. In 1961 he actually left the country in Nasution's charge as Army Commander, during one of those presidential "goodwill" forays in foreign capitals. He told a foreign diplomat on his return that "Nasution had no sense of opportunity" and that he "could be relied upon to remain true." Later events may have proved him to have been right.

In fact, General Nasution did make two attempts, neither of them very effective, to exploit opportunity. In 1952 he stormed the gates of Merdeka Palace with tanks, armoured cars and troops, his motive being not to obtain power but to put pressure on the President to scrap the noisy, time-wasting, appointed Parliament (later Nasution himself called this exercise "half-a-coup"). And as soon as the President was out of the country in 1961 Nasution made contact with the leaders of the Sumatran rebellion, who had been fighting a pathetically ineffectual war in the jungles, and suggested to them that they lay down their arms. The rebels, some of them Nasution's old comrades in arms during the guerilla war against the Dutch, asked him how they could even think of doing as he suggested in the face of the retribution they would meet with from Sukarno. Nasution then assured them that before the end of the year Sukarno would be "either under my thumb or out of the Presidency". They remonstrated, pointing out that Nasution had never shown any evidence of standing up to the President. "How could I?" argued Nasution. "As long as you remain in the jungle, I am vulnerable. The Bung is able to point to you as evidence of my failure. He asks how can

Indonesia become normal as long as the rebels are in the jungle. If you stop the rebllion you will be strengthening my hand against him."

The time set for his projected show of Army strength was December 1961, and the code word was the Indonesian equivalent of "Operation Big Show". The rebels did precede it by coming out of the jungle and Sukarno promptly clapped them in concentration camps where they were subjected to a "re-education in the principles of the Indonesian Revolution" – all Sukarno's writings and speeches dating from the early days to the development of the concept of Guided Democracy and the *Gotong Royong* (mutual cooperation) Parliament were read to them every day. And Sukarno did not remain unaware of the rumours of "Operation Big Show" which were floating about when he arrived back from abroad. He watched and waited for the first signs of it.

In November that year, as the deadline approached, tension mounted in Djakarta. Then Jawaharlal Nehru – acting on the advice of Krishna Menon – gave Sukarno the loophole he was searching for. India marched into Goa and took it over forcibly from the Portuguese who had held the colony for four hundred years. Sukarno joined the chorus of applause at the extinction of yet another pocket of colonialism in Asia, and stepped up his vocal campaign demanding the handing over of Irian Barat (then Dutch New Guinea). Within days, the invasion of Irian Barat seemed imminent. This was one issue on which all Indonesians felt alike. There was not the remotest chance of Operation Big Show being successful at a time when West Irian was so much in the air. Sukarno's side-show had captured the audience. Nasution's plans – his intentions rather – petered out. So, for the moment, did the vehemence of the Irian Barat campaign. At no time did Sukarno bring up the subject of Operation Big Show with Nasution. If he had, it would certainly have led to a showdown with the Army and this the President was anxious to avoid. But when the time came for his annual cabinet reshuffle – a device he used skilfully to keep his ministers in line – he kicked Nasution upstairs.

Nasution was deprived of his command of the Army and given the portfolio of Defence which, with the "Crush Malaysia" campaign hotting up, had less power than the job of Army Commander and much less than the portfolio of Foreign Affairs now held by Subandrio. Separated from his command, Nasution was soon cut off from the centre of public affairs. In the power game it is essential to be in the limelight. And Nasution could not stand the limelight. There is an Indonesian legend which makes the point neatly. A little boy was fishing when a horseman rode up and asked him whether he would share his rod and tackle. The boy and the horseman fished for an hour and when the sun was setting the horseman offered the boy a lift home. Instead of taking the boy to his parents' hut, the horseman took him to an enormous palace. The boy asked where they were going and the horseman replied that this was his home. He was the Ratu, the King. In the palace, the King asked the boy to sit beside him on his throne in the audience chamber and announced to his Ministers that he had decided to share his kingdom with the boy. The Ministers protested that they had served the king faithfully without reward, and asked what the boy had done to deserve this special mark of appreciation. The King replied: he shared his rod with me. But the Ministers argued that they would have been willing to share their rods with the King if only they had been fishing when he passed by. The King smiled sardonically and replied: "Ah, but this boy WAS fishing at the very moment I felt I would like to do some fishing. You were not. Half my kingdom will go to him. It is decided."

General Nasution became increasingly isolated from the President as well as from the Army, now under the command of General Yani. Characteristically, he enhanced this isolation by his solitary brooding for many months. By the time he had got over it, his isolation was complete. Yani and he were hardly on talking terms. Indonesians who had regarded Nasution as their white hope of the future, were alarmed by the extent of his aloofness and advised him to make and maintain contact with Yani and the Army commanders and to secure his place in the Cabinet by every means possible. Nasution made the gestures but they seemed hollow. He stretched out his hand to the generals, but in a lukewarm manner. He made the necessary noises about crushing Malaysia, oftener and more vehemently than Aidit himself, but it was quite evident that although it enabled him to avoid charges of being against the foreign policy of the President, no one was taken in by his verbal bellicosity. Even across the straits, the Malays he was apparently determined to chew and crush, still held to their notion that the only man in the upper reaches of the Indonesian power hierarchy they would trust was General Nasution. During the bitterest days of confrontation Tengku Abdul Rahman still spoke of him in the fondest terms. Much to Nasution's embarrassment, even British journalists and diplomats spoke of him openly in Djakarta as their blue-eyed boy. Their esteem sometimes threatened his position with the President, and Subandrio never passed up a chance to whisper that this was evidence of Nasution's lack of revolutionary ardour.

Nasution's charm of manner, his ability to speak Dutch and English, his reputation for financial probity and his evident preference for libertarian methods of governing people were the qualities that prompted foreign observers of the Indonesian scene to create the impression abroad that he was the likely successor to President Sukarno. In point of fact, very few Indonesians credited him with that potential. To succeed President Sukarno at the height of his power and glory, another giant was needed and Nasution never measured up. The fact that he was not a Javanese but a Sumatran reduced his stature as far as the Javanese generals and the intellectuals were concerned. Indonesia has indeed been unified by Sukarno but, as is the case in India – or in Britain – cultural and emotional parochialism are still powerful forces. In India Mr Kamaraj is still unthinkable as Prime Minister because he is a South Indian. Similarly, a Sumatran may be highly respected as a general or a cabinet minister but he has small chance of being acceptable as President in a country where traditionalism continues to be a major motivating factor.

Although General Yani and the late Admiral Eddie Martadinata* had great respect for Nasution as a human being they did not share their innermost thoughts with him. As the commanders moved farther and farther away from Nasution, Subandrio's influence and stature increased. By 1964 he had things going very much the way he wished. He had the President's ear and trust, he had built up an international reputation, he was influential in Peking, he had armed support in the Marine Corps, the Air Force and among the volunteers and he had ready access to the mass media – the newspapers and the radio. He was virtually Prime Minister, Foreign Minister and Home Minister and by 1965, the undisputed heir-apparent to the President.

The Army protested at various times and in varying degrees of frustration about being ignored in major decisions taken by the Cabinet. The generals, through their newly established newspapers – the *Berita Yudha* and *Angatan Bersendjata*, revealed their increasing alarm at the lopsidedness of NASAKOM in practice. Since all news had to be funnelled through Antara, the State News Agency which deliberately ignored "news" of interest to the Army, the public received only PKI-slanted information. The Army demanded "proportional representation" on the staff of Antara and the reinstatement of three non-communist directors of the news agency who had been sacked. In February 1965 the PKI succeeded in getting the President

*Killed in a helicopter crash in October 1966.

to ban twenty-one non-communist newspapers. The same pressure succeeded in removing sixty non-communist journalists from the membership of the PWI, the Indonesian Journalists Association. Since membership of the PWI was obligatory for all journalists, this order meant not only the loss of their jobs but also of their occupation. Like Rosihan Anwar, the proscribed editor of the *Pedoman*, they faced the prospect of having to make a bare living for themselves and their families by odd-jobbing as translators.

The PKI staff of Antara had begun to surpass themselves in their tendentiousness. The Army told the President that "progressive revolutionary parties* such as the religious parties, feel themselves harmed by certain reports by Antara". The newspaper war between the PKI-directed press and the Army-owned press became hotter as the year wore on. In June the Army newspaper *Angatan Bersendjata* declared: "Since the press is the main instrument of President Sukarno's fundamental doctrine of Pantjasila, it should be in the hands of GENUINE pantjasilaists." These statements clearly hinted at increasing cohesion between the Army and the religious groups: the reference to "genuine pantjasilaists" was directed against the PKI newspapermen who, as communists, could not subscribe sincerely to the first five principles of Pantjasila: allegiance to Allah, the One God.

The Army, more and more insulated from the centre of political power by Subandrio and by the PKI, sought a base of mass support in the religious groups who could be counted on to be hostile to the communists when the showdown came. President Sukarno's talent for tight-rope walking between these opposing forces was sorely tested during this period. He tried setting off one against the other but the

*The only parties permitted to exist were those who subscribed to the principles of the Indonesian Revolution. They were therefore "progressive". The Communists of course regarded them as "reactionary" as by definition: anyone who was religious, i.e., believed in God, could not possibly be "progressive".

entire structure was collapsing underneath him. He tried, for instance, to balance the preponderance of the PKI influence in the Antara News Agency by making regulations in late June 1965 to restrict the number of newspapers to the number of parties and "functional groups" (e.g. the Army) concerned with publications. This would have meant one paper for each faction and would have hit the PKI badly since the communists had by far the largest number of newspapers. But Subandrio and Aidit fought a rearguard action against this move and managed to have it shelved.

By July 1965 the PKI attack on the Army and the religious groups had become blatant. A carefully phased campaign was set afoot to create conditions under which the PKI would be able to rely on the weight of the masses against any attempt by the Army to take power when the momentarily expected death of the President occurred. For the first time the PKI called out its street armies to protest against the high cost of living that was now beginning to be intolerable to the urban population. Throughout the archipelago slogans were directed against high prices and profiteers. Suddenly it became dangerous for a white skinned person to walk about the streets. The economic ruin of Indonesia was blamed squarely on the *necolims* – this catchword no longer denoting neocolonialism and imperialism but, simply, white skin. Anyone with a white skin was inevitably a *necolim* or a *kabir* (Kapitalist Birokrat).

In East Java the communists launched open attacks against the Muslim ulamas, who were accused of mixing reactionary political theories into their religious teachings. In ever widening circles centred on Djakarta, Bandung, Semarang, Solo, Madiun, Malan, Surabaya, Makassar, Medan and Palembang local PKI cells and the communists who had filtered into the nationalist party, the PNI, instigated part-time bandits and anyone willing to make a little quick money to plunder what they could from people they thought to be *kabirs*.

Chapter V

EXPLODING DEMANDS

The PKI invented a term for this profiteer-hunting: *tundjuk hidung* (pointing the nose). The *Indonesian Herald*, the English language newspaper controlled by Dr Subandrio, explained the term as "an encouragement to the members of the community to help the government to identify persons who had become rich at the expense of society". The *Herald* announced that those who carried out this "patriotic duty" would receive "a promise from the government that the arms of the law [*sic*] will administer the long promised maximum penalty [death] to the guilty". The reporter went on: "This invitation to the *rakjat* [people] to exert social control on the enemies of state and society – these corruptors and capitalist bureaucrats are certainly dangerous enemies – stems from the belief that the common people can do the job more efficiently."

Such an invitation to loot with impunity could hardly be resisted by people living on the edge of starvation, driven panicky by the steep rise in prices of food and clothing. Bands of thugs started to raid farms and kiosks everywhere. Anyone who owned something visible – a paddy field, a banana plot, a papaya garden, a vegetable plantation, foodstuffs for sale or a few sticks of sugarcane to hawk about in the streets – came into the category of *kabirs*. The nose of the PKI was pointed at them. The farmers sought protection not from the police, who were under the control of Dr Subandrio, but from the Army. This was a long established tradition in Indonesia: since the early days of the struggle for independence the farming community had sought assistance and protection from the military commander in the area. The police were always regarded as being "on the other side" – the side of the oppressors, were they Dutch, Japanese or Indonesian. The Army sometimes inflicted summary punishment on the raiders but, more often than not, it could provide nothing but a sense of protection by its presence in the neighbourhood.

Not to be outdone by the communists who seemed to be succeeding in spreading fertile disquiet in the country, the nationalist leaders issued a call to their members to "beware of fake *mahaenists* (independent smallholders) who are really *kabirs* in disguise". Dr Ali Sastroamidjojo, the Chairman of the Nationalist Party, praised the Police Department for "not taking the side of these fake *mahaenists*."*

The reason for the concentrated attack on the *mahaenist* population of the villages was that it was the strongest repository of religious or spiritual faith. The *mahaenists* are the *santris*, the "believers". They believe in the oneness of God, they believe in the Prophet Muhammad, they believe in animistic rituals and propitiary practices, they believe in the rightness of their tradition and experience, they believe in the wisdom of their ulamas because they had been taught through the generations to respect their teachers, and they believe that their land had been given to them by God. They were not much concerned with Afro-Asianism, nor did they see the transformation of the world as an urgent duty; but they *were* concerned about their crops, the safety of their families and the stature of their President, and they saw it as a probability that the government was telling them the truth about their neighbours in Malaysia plotting with the white man to destroy what they had. Living at a low but presumably adequate level of subsistence, the *mahaenists*

*"*Mahaenism*" was a term invented by President Sukarno who saw in a small farmer named Mahaen he once met, the model he was seeking as the human base of the Indonesian economy. He described a *mahaenist* as "a person with small means; a little man with little ownership, little tools, sufficient to himself who works for no one and no one works for him. *Mahaenism* is Indonesian socialism in operation."

formed the most stable sector of the economy. This was the target of the PKI: to create widespread disorder among them in the rural areas; disorder which could then be used as a force which could be directed according to the will of the local PKI cell leaders and the communist wing of the PNI.

The attacks on the "reactionaries" were no longer vague and diffuse. The reactionaries were the "religionists", the "stupid believers in outmoded ideas", "the superstitious gulls who believe in supernatural phenomena". Such abuse always carefully avoided stating explicitly that belief in Allah was superstitious or outmoded. This would have brought on the PKI the wrath not only of the religious parties but also of the President who frequently protested and affirmed his faith in the One God and His Prophet, Muhammad. And this was not a risk worth taking.

As the year wore on, the atmosphere in Indonesia became increasingly charged with tension and apprehension. The raids on property became increasingly frequent and bold. Violent crimes were committed with growing ferocity and casualness. The street slogans became noisier and more brutal in character. There were more and more scribbled threats to hang opponents. Prices were rising at a faster rate than ever before. By August the dollar rate had long passed the 20,000 rupiah mark and was now careering along in the 30 thousands. By September 15 a dollar fetched 40,000. The currency situation was now obviously uncontrollable. The currency factory in Djakarta could not keep pace with the demand for notes.

Dr Subandrio told the opening session of the National Congress of Plantation Workers: "The time has now come to exterminate the capitalist bureaucrats, members of the so-called 'economic dynasty' and manipulators of State funds." D. N. Aidit, the leader of the PKI, told the same meeting: "The task of the working class at a time like this, when prices are rising and the situation is bad, is to step up the revolutionary offensive in all fields and develop the revolutionary situation towards its peak and thereby cut out the cancer from the body of the Indonesian Revolution."

The cry against high prices became louder and screechier. In the face of this accelerated crumbling of the economy, Indonesia's leaders had only two weapons: intensifying their own slogans calculated to create a local diversion, or reverting to the begging bowl. Dr Subandrio told a crowd in Menado: "Power must be in the hands of the people and it is you who will determine the destruction of the corruptors."

But people were apparently becoming less willing to be fobbed off by words and slogans, however high their source and however grandiloquent their expression. Housewives' groups began to band themselves together to stage protest marches in the cities demanding the immediate reduction of the price of rice, sugar, chillies and textiles. The students' movements also changed the burden of their slogans from politics to economics. President Sukarno coined another phrase for popular consumption: *Berdikari*, Self-Reliance. His Ministers went about the country preaching self-reliance as the most formidable weapon of the revolution. This was only another way of asking people to tighten their belts. 1965 was declared "The Year of Self-Reliance". On September 19 Dr Subandrio was reported thus:

"In the field of economy the imperialists are more in need of Indonesia than Indonesia of them. The imperialists without their progressive forces will see their standard of living decline. Indonesians, without the imperialists, on the other hand, will be in a position to improve their economy. Our economic experts must abandon the textbooks of the economic experts of Harvard, Columbia and Leyden. They will lose nothing by doing this. It is true that at present Indonesia is experiencing a big inflation. However, within a year, in line with a command from the President, it is expected that economic difficulties of all kinds will be overcome. This calls for the elimination of conventional thinking on the part of the nation's economists."

But all the talk of *berdikari* did not prevent a team of fifty politicians and officials from being sent to Peking and Pyong Yang to ask for more economic aid to tide over the current crisis. It is significant that Dr Subandrio who had made the arrangements for this visit recommended to the President that Dr Chairul Saleh, founder of the banned Body for the Promotion of Sukarnoism, should head the delegation. Chairul Saleh left on September 25, thus removing himself physically from the game of political musical chairs which was rapidly reaching its climax.*

The reaction of the people to the idea of self-reliance was not docile. Apparently they were not to be appeased any longer with alibis and promises of jam tomorrow, jam the day after and jam next week. They asked for rice and chillies and clothing *today*, at prices which they could afford. The temper of the city population was becoming so edgy that President Sukarno himself decided to come forward with an explanation of the economic crisis:

"Only a nation with exploding demands, aspirations and ideals to develop its future can become a great nation. I am very grateful to God Almighty that the Indonesian people have exploding demands, aspirations and ideals for its future . . . The Indonesian Revolution has now completed its first stage of achieving national democracy. We now have reached the second stage of the Revolution. In implementing this second stage we should greet with joy the rising demands of the people, which lately have become exploding demands, because we ourselves have turned the Indonesian people into a people with goals and demands . . ."

*Indonesian intellectuals like to speculate about what Chairul Saleh's destiny would have been had he been in Djakarta at the time of the *coup d'état* instead of being in far-away Peking. The likelihood is that he would have found it opportune to denounce the PKI and Subandrio and join with the Army in its campaign to eradicate the "foreign elements" – meaning the communist Chinese – accused of engineering the conspiracy.

The PKI leaders who cheered him lustily when this statement was made knew with sardonic certitude that these exploding demands would before long blow up in the President's face.

Chapter VI

A "BANTING-STIR"

The tension in Djakarta in the middle of 1965 was intensified by international developments. Radio Djakarta and the press pumped out information about events in Malaysia, Vietnam and on the Kashmir border which heightened expectancy and the sense of crisis. In August 1965 Singapore broke away from Malaysia after a series of wordy disputes between the Alliance Party in Kuala Lumpur and the Singapore government. Indonesia hailed this as a vindication of its view that Malaysia was a hasty piece of political jerrymandering by the neocolonialist British and their Asiatic flunkeys. The Indonesian Foreign Office announced its certainty that Sabeh and Sarawak, the two other components which had extended the Federation of Malaya into Malaysia, would soon follow the example of Singapore and walk out or get themselves kicked out, leaving Malaya as it was before all the fuss started. When, after the first tears of regret and commiseration had been shed by the Tengku and Mr Lee Kuan Yew the Prime Minister of Singapore, barbed words began to fly once more across the Johore Straits, Djakarta was delighted. Dr Subandrio even dropped a calculated aside or two suggesting the possibility of Indonesia's giving early recognition to Singapore in order to increase the Tengku's chagrin.

The decision of the United States to drop bombs in North Vietnam territory gave the PKI daily reason to bring out its street demonstrators and keep them on the boil. The attacks on *necolim* – that is to say white-skinned – visitors were now justified on the ground that they were the representatives of the nation that was bringing death and destruction to fellow Asians in Vietnam. *Betjak* drivers referred to "*necolim* passengers" and swimming-pool attendants at the Hotel Indonesia complained about the rowdiness of "*necolim* children" splashing about in the bath. Massive PKI demonstrations demanded the expulsion of the *necolim* from Vietnam, and KIAPMA posters heralding the forthcoming Conference on Foreign Bases sponsored by Dr Subandrio, depicted the people of Indonesia slaughtering the *necolim* with *kris*, long bladed *goloks* and farming rakes.

The air was so highly charged that foreign events had an immediate impact on the nerves of the man in the street in Djakarta. In July expectancy was high about the Afro-Asian meeting in Algiers called to take stock ten years after the Bandung conference. Dr Subandrio told the people that this meeting would show how Indonesia had begun to "succeed in its sacred duty of transforming the world". The people of Africa and Asia would revolt against the Oldefos (Old Established Forces) at Algiers. The United Nations Organisation established in "the most imperialistic of the *necolim* countries" would be deserted by the Africans and Asians who would then foregather in 1966 at the CONEFO (Conference of New Emerging Forces) to be held in Djakarta. Dr Subandrio demanded from the people a "spiritual mandate" which President Sukarno and he could take with them to Algiers to purge the Afro-Asian bloc of imperialistic flunkeys, who were, of course, Malaysia and her supporter, India. Unfortunately for Dr Subandrio, the host to the Asians and Africans in Algiers – President Ben Bella – was overthrown by Colonel Boumedienne a few days before the start of the meeting, when the procedural preliminaries had already commenced.

Subandrio's reactions were a mixture of disappointment and relief. Algiers was to have been the stage for his speech on the end of the United Nations and the beginnings of a new world body centred round Djakarta, Peking, Pyong

Yang and Pnom Penh, supported by the new African States. The leadership of the Third World, the massive two thirds of the world with undeveloped economies and substandard living conditions, would have been the prize at Algeria. The mantle of Jawaharlal Nehru was under the hammer. There were many contenders. China as a great power was not in the bidding. But there were Nasser, Nkrumah, Ben Bella, Fidel Castro, and President Sukarno, each of whom had shown the spirit and ability to thumb their noses at the *necolim*. Subandrio was to be the mouthpiece and strategist for this attempt. But by the time the officials and Foreign Ministers arrived in Algiers, it had become clear that two of Indonesia's most fervent hopes were already dashed: Malaysia and the USSR, whose admission to the conference Indonesia was eager to oppose,* were certain to be admitted. Ben Bella, as host, was not going to risk a walk-out by India, Ceylon and some African countries who had supported the USSR and Malaysia. Pakistan, for instance, was in a strange bind: President Ayub Khan was willing to oppose the admission of the Tengku but not prepared to bar the USSR. They would both have been admitted had the conference been held – a blow to Indonesia's prestige, since the decision to quit the UN had been taken on the ground of Malaysia's admission to one of the temporary seats on the Security Council. As for Indonesia's resolution asking the Afro-Asian bloc to quit the UN and join the rival world body being planned between Djakarta and Peking, there would not have been the remotest possibility of its success. Subandrio's timing had been atrocious: apart from political considerations, the notion of the Africans quitting the UN when Quaison-Sackey – a Ghanaian – was President of the UN was ludicrous.

Subandrio told his Foreign Office Staff in Djakarta that the postponement of the conference to November was a

*Indonesia had opposed the admission of the USSR at all Afro-Asian gatherings since Dr Subandrio began promoting the Djakarta-Peking alliance.

relief because "*necolim* influence" was "still powerful in the AA bloc". But simultaneously his disappointment was profound because he saw in the breakdown of the Algiers meeting the end of the effectiveness of the Afro-Asian conference as an instrument. He told his officials of his conviction that the November meeting, too, would become a shambles and that they must now pin their hopes on the Conference of New Emerging Forces planned for 1966 in Djakarta.

The new regime in Algeria was very anxious that the postponed conference should be held before the 1965 was out. By September the chances of its being able to meet seemed fairly good. Then Subandrio intensified his efforts to prevent the admission of Malaysia, India and the Soviet Union. When the war between India and Pakistan broke out in September, Indonesia abandoned even the thin veil of politeness towards India, who had given the world the ideal of neutralism but had, according to the Foreign Office in Djakarta, "betrayed the progressive principles which she had espoused at Bandung by supporting a *necolim* creation such as the so-called 'Malaysia'."

With the aid of the PKI, Subandrio put on a brave show of anti-Indian feeling in Java and Sumatra soon after the war began in earnest across the cease-fire line in Kashmir. The Air India office in Djakarta was ransacked and burned down. The Indian consulate in Medan, North Sumatra, was "taken over" by a PKI youth organisation on September 13. The Antara Agency reported:

> "Thousands of youths Monday noon took over the Indian Consulate and Information Services building in Medan. The action was described as a solid proof of Indonesia's solidarity with the Kashmiris and Pakistanis. The demonstrators hoisted the red and white flag after pulling down the Indian colours. Governor of North Sumatra com-

menting on the demonstrations said that the action of the youth was staged at the exact time . . ."

On September 21 thousands of "veterans" demonstrated outside the Indian Embassy in Djakarta. Their slogans expressed sympathy with Pakistan and attacked India for supporting Malaysia. On the same day the Praesidium of the Cabinet decided to place "all interests and property constituting units for trade or shops of Indian nationals in Indonesia under government supervision."

The tone and flavour of another report by Antara's Karachi correspondent indicate the sense of involvement in world drama that kept the populace in Djakarta excitedly preoccupied in the last few days before the beginning of the end of Sukarno:

> Karachi September 24: "Thousands of angry youths recently held demonstrations in Karachi, Dacca and Lahore in protest of UN decisions and also American and British support of Indian aggression against Pakistan. Carrying posters of the Great Leader of the Indonesian Revolution, Bun Karno, Mao Tse Tung, Chou en Lai, Liu Shao Chi and the Shahinshah of Iran, the demonstrators, unable to control their anger toward the American and British for their support of Indian aggression, rushed at the USIS and BIS building destroyed furnitures and broke glasses [*sic*] of the buildings. Books were thrown out of the buildings and burned. The demonstrators then headed for the buildings of the United Nations, American and Indian Embassies and broke all the windows to pieces."

The inclusion of the United Nations in the report of the wrath of the Karachi mob was a bit of "fumigation" on the part of the Antara news desk in Djakarta, which had recently received orders to give the UN the same treatment as that given to the Americans and the British in the agency's reports. Meanwhile Dr Subandrio was building up his case against India abroad through the foreign missions. A Special Report of the *Indonesian Herald*, datelined Djakarta, told readers on September 25 that:

> A number of Muslim countries are reported to be initiating a move to have India barred from the forthcoming Afro-Asian Conference in Algiers. These countries had already sent instructions to their delegates to the preparatory committee in Algiers to "sound out the view" of their colleagues. Similar soundings were also reported to have been made in a number of key capitals in Asia and Africa.
>
> Here in Djakarta, it is strongly believed, that President Sukarno has also been approached. It is not yet known whether this new development also transpired during the recent meeting between the Head of State and Foreign Minister Subandrio when they discussed the so-called "letters from abroad".

The caginess of the writing, the fact that it originated from Djakarta, its timing, the vagueness of "a number" (twice), the reference to the reporter's ignorance as to whether this subject had been discussed by Sukarno and Subandrio, and the care with which it is said that these moves were "initiated" outside, make it abundantly likely that the story was inspired in Djakarta, probably by Dr Subandrio himself. His hand is more plainly visible in the text which followed:

> "Political observers in the capital pointed out that India had indeed acted rather 'strangely' of late. It appeared that the Shastri government had adopted the role of trouble-maker rather than solidarity-promoter in recent African-Asian conferences. They recalled that last June, India and 'Malaysia' – the *necolim* Siamese twins – had worked closely together at the Commonwealth Prime

Ministers Conference to have the Algiers meeting postponed by means of an appeal concocted in London. When this failed, India tried to have the present Organisation Committee disbanded, thereby making the convening of a second African-Asian conference more difficult if not impossible. These observers also pointed out that last June, India had smuggled into Algiers a number of 'Malaysian' officials as 'advisors' to its delegation."

One observer, however, commented that India may voluntarily choose to stay away from Algiers in order to avoid all-out condemnation for its aggression against Pakistan . . .

The same report gave clear signs of the intention of the Sukarno-Subandrio combination to drum up support for the establishment of the rival world body they were planning to establish after the Algiers meeting:

"The prestige of the United Nations has sunk to its lowest ebb in the eyes of the African-Asian world, especially in the Muslim countries. They have come to realise that they could not rely on the world organisation when their security and religion were threatened by a country in friendship and alliance with the *necolim* powers. The fact that the world organisation had openly sided with India and had rescued the country from total defeat at the hands of Pakistani troops came as a cruel reminder of the firm *necolim* domination over the United Nations."

Another Antara report reflected the growing involvement of Indonesia in the Indo-Pakistan conflict and revealed that the anti-Indian stand of Djakarta had originated largely from India's refusal to support Indonesia's confrontation against Malaysia:

"Karachi Sept. 24: Pakistani official circles and press last Monday strongly resented 'Malaysia's' pro-India stand in the Security Council and for the first time openly denounced the neo-colonialist project as a colonialist project. Usually Pakistani leaders and the press avoided to use critical remarks towards 'Malaysia's' dispute with Indonesia."

Dr Subandrio had never yet succeeded in winning the trust or respect of the Muslim parties, whom he regarded as the worst reactionaries in Indonesia. Now he was able to use the Indo-Pakistan war to arouse their sympathy on his side. In his public addresses and press statements he constantly referred to the fact that Pakistan was a Muslim state under attack by non-Muslims, although one of the notable features of the Indo-Pakistan war was that neither side allowed it to deteriorate into a religious war so that the widely feared religious holocaust in East Pakistan and West Bengal never occurred.

On September 23 a joint working conference of the Nahdatul Ulama Party (the party of the Islamic religious teachers) instructed all its branch organisations to form immediately a corps of volunteers to be sent to Pakistan. In a formal announcement the NU leaders said: "This is in the framework of implementing the command of the Champion of Islam and Great Leader of the Revolution, Bung Karno, in extending support to Muslim Pakistan."

While leaders of the country were turning their attention to conflict and crisis abroad, the cost of living crisis had begun to spread into the villages which had hitherto managed to rest on subsistence production. Farmers associations formed by the PNI and the PKI began to murmur about the cost of simple household articles. The President was advised by Minister of Agriculture Sadjarwo that it was time for the rural people to be given a pep talk to prevent them from "turning against the Revolution". In the last week of September the Great Leader therefore addressed a gathering of 12,000 farmers and according to the Antara record:

" . . . stressed that the increasing prices of commodities constitute an intricate problem which must be solved in its integrity [*sic*]. To lower the prices such factors as increased production, changes in menu and eradication of swindlers and *necolim* are involved. Indonesian farmers, as a main pillar of the Revolution, must always stay in the forefront of the line."

When members of the Farmers Union asked what plans the government had to bring down prices, the President's reply was characteristic:

"I have discussed this matter with members of the Supreme Advisory Council. None of the distinguished members of that Council have volunteered to assume the responsibility of lowering the prices within a year. They realise the complexity of the problem to be faced. There are swindlers to be dealt with. But this is only a minor part of the causes. The insufficient condition of the infrastructure and the struggle against the *necolim* are more important factors which effect the high prices. Those who say the swindling practice is the main cause are really launching cheap propaganda."

This "realism" was by no means as guileless as it sounds. The man in the street and the ordinary farmer, loathe to blame the government of the Great Leader for their predicament, were openly accusing the retail traders of profiteering in essential goods. The bulk of this trade was in the hands of the Chinese of whom there are nearly 3,000,000 left in Indonesia. As the government swung increasingly to the left and came more and more under the influence of the Peking-PKI line, the Chinese population, always vulnerable to attack as a minority, gave considerable financial support to the PKI. Beparki, the Chinese residents' political party, made large annual donations to the PKI. This was protection money, but they paid it readily enough as long as no awkward questions were asked about the source of their funds and the prices they charged. Sukarno and Subandrio were anxious therefore to shift the blame for the poverty of the Indonesian people on to the *necolim* abroad. Subandrio, in fact, ever more skilfully, provided them with a whipping-boy with a local habitation and a name: the liberals. He told the crowds in Djakarta on that same day that "all elements which could not follow the course of the Revolution should be eliminated by the people. We must remain non-cooperative with people still suffering from liberalism and capitalism, people having liberal-democratic ideas still".

Indonesia was ripe for a change – for what they called a "*banting-stir*", a drastic change. Sukarno welcomed it as the second stage of the Revolution: the revolution of exploding demands. There were whispers about Djakarta that the PKI was planning its own brand of "*banting-stir*". A head-on clash between the Army and the PKI seemed inevitable.

Aidit, the Communist leader, issued a statement to the press stressing that "the only way to solve the present economic crisis is by way of operating on the cancer of society – namely the capitalist bureaucrats, economic adventurers and corruptors known as the three evils of the cities". Mixing the metaphor, he went on to say that these three groups "constitute the parasite of the fertile tree of the Revolution with its thick foliage. These three evils must be retooled [eliminated] from the leadership of the State apparatus, politics, and culture and others [*sic*]."

No one in Indonesia who read these remarks could have possibly missed the significance of the innuendos: the canker in the State was the non-communist two-third of the NASAKOM cabinet – the Army and the Religious parties. The "others" referred to General Nasution who was Defence Minister. The reference to "culture" was directly aimed at the Nahdatul Ulama, the foremost religious political party.

Meanwhile the Armed Forces were preparing to celebrate

their 20th anniversary on October 5. The Army command announced that the purpose of the exercise was "to increase vigilance and integrate the Indonesian armed forces". Rear Admiral R. Sumengkar told reporters that the President would inspect a massive parade. He also revealed that manoeuvres had been planned in Tandjung Priok, the harbour area in Djakarta. His words are significant in the context of the events that occurred a few days later: "The theme of the manoeuvre is to recapture Djakarta after it has been occupied by the enemy. The operation necessary to recapture Djakarta will be made by a team of marines, a detachment of frogmen, a detachment of RPKAD [ground based paratroopers], a detachment of the Mobile Brigade, squadrons of helicopters, squadrons of the Army's troop-carrying aircraft."

The Chief of Staff of the Armed Forces at Merdeka Barat was reported by the newspapers to "be reflecting an air of watchful waiting". He told the newsmen: "We must remain on the alert more than ever before. True we have been engaged in confrontation for more than two years now but today the problems are much more complicated."

The stage was being set for the action that was to change the history of Indonesia overnight. But the protagonist of this vast drama was busy reciting lines from some other play, for some other time, in some other setting. At a ceremony held at Merdeka Palace to install a new Inspector General of Police, Sukarno declared: "If the fate of mankind was once determined by Washington and Moscow it is now determined by Washington, Moscow, Peking AND Djakarta. We have now emerged from being a nation of coolies into a nation which determines the history of mankind."

Chapter VII

INTIMATIONS OF MORTALITY

Such was the mood and temper of the man whom everyone involved in the power struggle believed to be on the point of death. As early as August 1964 there had been rumours floating about Djakarta that President Sukarno, then sixty-three, was mortally ill. Various guesses were offered as diagnoses. An American observer keenly interested in Indonesian developments and extremely knowledgeable about the country, reported that he was convinced that the President was suffering from General Paralysis of the Insane. His diagnosis was based on his observation of symptoms of chronic paranoia alternating with manic depression in Sukarno's public and private conduct. A physician who had attended the President told his former associates in the banned Socialist Party that Sukarno would not live beyond a year or two at the most – and that only if he laid off women and took things easy. The most widespread belief was that Sukarno was suffering from progressive kidney failure – that one of his kidneys was already defunct and the other rapidly deteriorating. There was support for this theory in the recollections of his associates during the Japanese occupation, who clearly remembered that Bung Karno even as a young man suffered from kidney stones. And in his autobiography – written recently – he says plainly: "The only thing Tchakrabirawa (the Palace Regiment) can't guard is my health. I have one kidney that's a stone factory and the other my doctors watch minutely as if it were under a microscope."

Sukarno scoffed at the rumour-mongers when he

appeared at mass meetings and on television, but as the year wore on his condition did deteriorate. On December 14 *The Times*, London, reported:

> Kuala Lumpur – December 13: The Indonesian Government today admitted that President Sukarno is ill. Radio Djakarta, in a report from the Presidential Palace at Bogor, forty miles away, said the sixty-four year old President was "walking with a limp, from a swollen leg, and looked tired from overwork". President Sukarno, who is suffering from a kidney complaint, has been under treatment in Vienna and by four doctors from Peking who are specialists in acupuncture.

The fact that Radio Djakarta, a rigidly government controlled organ, had made this announcement added pace and credibility to the rumours of the President's impending death.

It was at this time that Dr Chairul Saleh made his bid for the rank of heir-apparent to the Presidency. Chairul Saleh, Chairman of the MPRS or Peoples Consultative Assembly, and Third Deputy Prime Minister, had his own destiny to fulfil. In 1955 he had consulted a celebrated German seer called Madame Farida who had foretold that on his return to Indonesia he would "make a comeback and become a highly placed person". She had added: "Chairul Saleh is destined, if only for a day, to reach the highest office in the land." Chairul Saleh who, as leader of the pseudo-Trotskyite Murba party which the President had banned out of existence, had opposed Sukarno so hotly, made peace with him in 1957 and was given Cabinet rank as Minister for Veteran Affairs. Later he worked himself up to become Chairman of the MPRS, the highest legislative body in the country deriving its authority from the 1945 Constitution. A few years earlier Chairul Saleh extended a "special invitation" to Madame Farida to visit Djakarta. Asked if her prophecy still held true she replied: "*Immer dasselbe*". But a wan smile accompanied the continuation of the prophecy. "When Chairul Saleh reaches the highest office he will be involved in a blood bath."

When news of the President's illness was officially confirmed Chairul Saleh got his campaign under way. He decided to exploit Sukarno's egotism and, at the same time, undermine the influence of D. N. Aidit, the PKI and Subandrio. He announced the establishment of the political organisation already referred to, called The Body for the Promotion of Sukarnoism. He let it be known that the purpose of the BPS was to "promote Bung Karno's ideas and policies and to enshrine them among his friends so that they will be preserved intact after the Bung's death". He claimed that he had the support of General Nasution, Adam Malik (Minister of Commerce) and General Yani (Army Commander), and openly stated that his party's policy was anti-communist. The BPS, as stated earlier, was shortlived. Under pressure from the PKI, the President banned it on the grounds that it "distracted the people from the course of the Revolution". But brief as its life was, the formation of BPS provided the first indication of the way the people near and around the centre of power were going to line up when the Great Vacancy occurred.*

The trouble with astrological charts of the destiny of political leaders is that counter-predictions with equally rosy promises are available to their rivals. Dr Subandrio, despite his intellectual hauteur, and even Aidit, the Marxist-Leninist, the dialectical materialist, each had his own tame astrologer who had cleared his path to the peak

*As it happened, Chairul Saleh found himself ranged alongside the PKI and Dr Subandrio and against his associates in the BPS when the Army wrested power from the President on March 11, a year later. On March 14 Chairul Saleh made a national call to the people over Radio Djakarta "on behalf of the President, the Great Leader of the Revolution, the Sole Interpreter of the Revolution, etc., etc., etc.". A day later he was put under house arrest to be brought to trial for "corrupt practices". Perhaps Madame Farida did know a thing or two.

of power. Subandrio's horoscope gave him, according to his own seer, a head start against all comers.

Moderate political elements in Djakarta, the remains of the old Socialist Party, the uncommitted intellectuals and those whose centre of gravity was Islam or Christianity became more and more terrified of the possibility that Subandrio would succeed Sukarno. There was even the likelihood that Sukarno would nominate Subandrio as his successor before he became too ill to rule, and would actually see him snugly installed as President before his own death. This fear was of course shared by the extreme rightists of the banned Darul Islam and Masjumi organisations. Many of these people had worked with Subandrio before and some even had an admiration for his quick mind and nimble tongue. Their terror was not so much of him as of the means he would have to use in order to secure and retain the Presidency. Against the Army he had no chance whatever without the massive support of the PKI. And once in, Subandrio would not be able to balance the conflicting forces as Sukarno had done for so many years. Before long Subandrio and Indonesia would be in the communist bag.

General Ibrahim Adjie, until recently Commander of the famous Siliwangi Division which destroyed the PKI rebellion at Madiun in 1948, spoke openly about his fears: there was no officer in the Army, he said, who was not deeply concerned about what the PKI's hold on Subandrio implied. Adjie felt that the PKI would use Subandrio much more cynically and effectively than he was planning to use it. Subandrio was to be the Kerensky of Indonesia. Adjie told the press that he and the Army intended to prevent this from happening. "We knocked them out before. We knock them again if necessary."

The situation was becoming so tense that the President had to hold several *musjawarrahs* where rival political factions could meet together, eat together, and settle their differences with the aid of the catalytic powers of the President. Each of these brotherly jamborees ended with the radio and press announcing that each party and person present had "pledged their allegiance to the Great Leader Bung Karno and had promised to bury their differences for the sake of the Glorious Indonesian Revolution". But there was never a question in anyone's mind about the sincerity of these pledges, since the key to the turbulence was the common expectation of the early death of the President.

As the Armed Forces Day, October 5, drew nearer, rumours of an army *coup d'état* were rife. There were two possible dates suggested for such an event – October 5 or November 10 (Heroes' Day, when Indonesia commemorates those who died for the Revolution). When this rumour came round the second time, as might have been expected, it had a new dimension: the Army Generals were conspiring with the CIA to take power from Bung Karno by force of arms. The US Seventh Fleet was preparing to go into action. It was not difficult to guess where this story originated or, in the light of the events that took place soon after the rumours began circulating, the reason for it.

An Antara report dated September 25 pointed to the preparations being made by the PKI:

> Djakarta, September 25: Front Pemuda [Youth Front] headquarters here expressed high appreciation to the step taken by the Djakarta Raya Police to "open its doors for twenty-four hours" to receive reports from the public on irresponsible activities by capitalist bureaucrats, economic dynasty elements, pilferers of public wealth and corrupters . . . [It] also pointed to statements made by *nasakom* [nationalist, religious and communist] leaders who had asked "what are we waiting for?" in facing these corruptors. This should be interpreted by the youths as an order to launch mass and revolutionary actions throughout the country together with the patriotic in-

struments of the revolution, particularly the Police Force and the Public Prosecution, against these corruptors, capitalist-bureaucrats, pilferers and charlatans "and drag them to the gallows or to be shot in public".

Dr Subandrio's complicity in these preparations was made clear by his statement of the same day to Antara: "The time has come to exterminate the capitalist bureaucrats."

The tempo of events rose to fever pitch when people noticed that Professor Dr Wu Chieh Ping, the head of the team of Chinese doctors from Peking attending on Sukarno, had now taken to accompany his patient everywhere he went.

Chapter VIII

THE NIGHT OF SEPTEMBER 30

On the evening of September 30 President Sukarno was speaking at a convention of the Association of Indonesian Technicians held in the Djakarta stadium, flanked by the National Monument which is topped by the twenty-foot-high flame of gold: a symbolic juxtaposition, since this was to be the meeting at which the torch went out for him.

The President was clad characteristically in the uniform of Commander in Chief. He had his black *pitji* on his head and dark glasses against the glare of the stadium lights. He spoke of the need for skilled technicians to fulfil the promise of the second stage of the Indonesian Revolution, to transform the material resources of the country into goods which satisfy the "exploding demands" of the people. He stressed, as usual, the necessity for Indonesian engineers and technicians to avoid falling victim to the ideological machinations of the *necolim*. He reminded his audience to be proud of the fact that Indonesia was now able to produce her own atomic bomb by dint of the efforts of one of Indonesia's own physicists who had arrived at his knowledge from his own researches, starting from scratch, without any help from physicists abroad . . .

Sukarno had spoken for one hour and ten minutes when his voice faltered. He stopped and left the rostrum, seeming to limp. His aides were heard calling out, apparently for the attendant doctors. Dr Wu, the chief of the medical team from Peking, hurried to his side. The President, apparently in a state of collapse, was taken to a small room in the stadium and was closeted with his doctors for about an hour.

Pandemonium broke out in the audience and many tried to storm the rostrum to find out how ill the President was. Some of the crowd began to weep. One woman started a panic by shouting: "The President is dead." The cry was taken up and the Tchakrabirawa guards had to appeal for calm. They were not very successful. The news of the President's condition was already buzzing through the city and the rumour that he was dead had sent people scampering off to break the news to their friends.

It was, however, a false alarm. After receiving medical attention, the President, who freely confesses that he derives more benefit from addressing a crowd than from all the doctors around him, returned to the rostrum and continued his speech to a relieved but still bewildered audience.

That should have been the end of that incident – an episode in the life of an ageing, ailing revolutionary – but for the fact that the President's death, expectantly awaited by many claimants for his power, had been ordained as the signal for a train of momentous events to start moving.

One of the VIPs present at the meeting did not rush onto the platform or go backstage to see what was happening. This was D. N. Aidit, the leader of the PKI. He made for the exit and was never seen in public again. He had, as we shall see, a significant hand in the happenings of that night. But the man who set them in motion, Lieutenant Colonel Untung, Commander of the elite Tchakrabirawa Regiment – the President's Praetorian guard – was not present in the stadium when Sukarno collapsed. When the news reached him, Untung was at his headquarters not far from Merdeka Palace. Believing that the President was dead or dying, he pressed the button and the *Gerkang* (Movement) of September 30 got under way.

Squads of Tchakrabirawa troops in jeeps and trucks were despatched to kidnap eight generals and take them to the air force base at Halim about fifteen miles from the centre of the town. They were to be held there until further orders were given about their disposal. Untung told the men who later arrested him that his "instructions were limited to kidnapping". The action against the eight generals was to commence after midnight. This operation was to be divided between platoons of the Tchakrabirawa Regiment and the Communist Youth Front organisation who had been trained for the Crush Malaysia build-up and who, according to Untung, had been selected for this action on the grounds of their "special devotion to the NASAKOM idea of Bung Karno". Each detail was provided with trucks, jeeps and guns. Each one of them was given a separate timing for carrying out the action – a schedule drawn up with meticulous researches into the habitual personal timetables followed by the generals. General Yani, the Army Commander, was at the head of the list; General Nasution, the Defence Minister, was next; General Suharto was down for 2 a.m. and the others at various times between 3 and 5 a.m.

Mrs Yani's story of the events of that night spread through the country within a few hours of their occurrence. She had been an eye-witness and was able to say enough to convince everyone that the worst had happened to the Army's top men. Mrs Yani reported that soon after midnight her entire family was awakened by the sound of a shot at the door. Some Tchakrabirawa troops with guns had blown off the lock with a pistol shot and walked in to the drawing-room. Her husband went out in his pyjamas to ask them the meaning of their action. Mrs Yani and some of her children (she has eight) heard General Yani asking the Tchakrabirawa troops rather brusquely to explain themselves. They replied that they had been sent by President Sukarno to bring the General to the Palace. Yani, obviously incredulous, asked how they had got past the guard outside his house. There was no answer. Yani refused to accompany them to the Palace but said he would go there on his own. They tried to grab him and a short scuffle followed. One of the men shot the General and, in the presence of his wife and children, his body was wrapped in a carpet from the floor and carried away in a truck waiting outside.

General S. Parman, who ranked as First Assistant to General Yani, was not so fortunate as his chief. He was not dead when he was taken away. *The Berita Yudha Minggu* published the story of Mrs Parman on October 17. Here is an abridged version of the report:

> On September 30 General Parman had gone to bed as usual at midnight. At four o'clock, hearing a noise outside, he got up, thinking there were some thieves around. When he came out from his house, he saw armed men wearing the uniform of the Tchakrabirawa Regiment (about twenty of them).
>
> "Ah, you are from Tchakra?" The General said.
>
> "Yes, *Pak* [Father]. We have been ordered by the Supreme Commander [President Sukarno] to fetch you."
>
> "The situation is critical?" the General asked.
>
> "Yes *Pak*, very critical," was the answer.
>
> The General then went back to his bedroom to dress and the men followed him inside. The General told his wife to tell General Yani about the whole thing. But when they were all outside again, he noticed the men were taking his telephone away. His wife was not immediately suspicious because the General had often been thus called away by General Yani when there was anything important. A quarter of an hour later General Harjono's wife came crying to their house and asked for General Parman, her own husband having already been taken away.

On October 11 the *Angatan Bersendjata* published the account of the wife of General Pandjaitan about the drama which took place at her house in the early hours of October 1. Here is a brief translation:

"According to the general's family, just before dawn,

the ferocious group of the *Gestapu* came to General Pandjaitan's house. His nephew, Albert Neiborho, who was his "personal guard" tried to stop them. A quarrel was heard, then Albert was shot. General Pandjaitan, wearing his full uniform, was seen with his hands up. He was shot in front of his door and his body was carried to a truck which was waiting in the street."

The Tchakrabirawa and Pemuda squads engaged in this operation took six generals from their houses that night: Lieutenant-General Achmad Yani, Major-General S. Parman, Brigadier-General Pandjaitan, Major-General Suprapto (Second Deputy Army Commander), Major-General Harjono (Third Deputy Commander) and Brigadier-General Sutojo (Inspector, Military Tribunals). Yani and Harjono were dead by the time they were thrown into the trucks. Pandjaitan was gravely wounded but was probably alive when he reached Halim, to which they were all taken. The others had to endure much before dying.

At Halim air base there was great excitement by 3 a.m. when the body of General Yani was brought in. The *Pemuda Rakjat*, young men and women of the PKI youth movement who had been rampaging through the country for many weeks already, had been told by their leaders: "Get to Halim if you want some excitement." When they heard the news of the President's collapse at the stadium, they piled into trucks which took them to Halim. Among them were members of the Gerwani,* the PKI's women's movement.

Ever since that night Indonesia has been humming with stories of months of training for the perverse bacchanal of blood that occurred that night. There are detailed accounts of obscene oath-taking and blood ceremonies gone through by the young communist women of the Gerwani in preparation for it. Whether these stories are true or not is not

*GERWANI: Another acroayun composed of GERKANG (Movement) and Wanita (woman).

important. What is important is that true, or only partially true, or false, they were believed by millions of people *and by the Army.* This was one of the major causes of the revulsion against the PKI which eventually caused its proscription and the downfall of President Sukarno from his hitherto inaccessible perch of power.

There is no doubt that the generals' bodies were mutilated, and brutally so. One of the members of the Gerwani who took part in what went on that night, Mrs Djamilah, a fifteen-year-old wife of a PKI member, gave the *Djakarta Daily Mail* a participant's evidence of the events:

> "Small knives and razor blades were distributed. I only got a razor blade. From afar we saw a thickset man wearing sleeping clothes, hands bound with red cloth and eyes also covered with red cloth. The platoon leader commanded us to beat up that person, then to cut his private parts. The first to start the beating and cutting we saw to be S. and Mrs Satro, leaders of the Tandjung Priok branch of Gerwani. Then followed other comrades . . . Finally I myself joined in the torture. All the 100 women did likewise and were witnesses . . . the victim was shot three times, then fell down, but was not yet dead. A green-uniformed person wearing crooked white bars on the shoulder ordered the actions, stabbing at the victim's private parts and cutting these parts and the body until he died."

Mrs Djamilah volunteered this information, explaining that she was three months pregnant and that she had been revolted by the horrors she had witnessed and participated in at Halim. She had not been present when the bodies were disposed of but had heard they had been thrown into a well nearby, and could not say more. She was arrested and imprisoned until she could be tried.

Chapter IX

PLOT AND COUNTERPLOT

GESTAPU: that is what the Indonesians call what took place on the night of September 30 – the swift and chaotic events which changed the whole pattern of history in Indonesia. With the Indonesian flair for telescoping initials and making up explosive slogans, somebody invented GESTAPU from "*Gerkang*" (Movement), September, and *Tigapolu* (thirty), simultaneously packing into the new word all the connotations of Nazi secrecy, violence and flouting of fundamental human decency. The word now arouses the same feelings in Indonesia as the burning of the Reichstag did in Germany or Guy Fawkes' plot did in Seventeenth Century Britain. But what precisely happened in detail no one can yet say. There are as many versions and as much speculation as there were about the circumstances of John F. Kennedy's assassination.

Since no Indonesian was ideologically or emotionally uninvolved, no independent body like the Earl Warren Commission, which investigated the Kennedy assassination, could have been appointed to collect and assess the evidence. Besides, President Sukarno, the only man who could have set up such an enquiry, was himself suspected of involvement in some aspects of the affair. Even the professors at the University of Djakarta and men who had had sound legal training, when discussing the GESTAPU soon allow their wishes to sire their thoughts and become deeply embroiled in justifying or denouncing not the events of September 30, but their political consequences.

There are, however, certain known and indisputable

facts connected with the events of that night and the days and months that followed. There are also various versions of some events which are less clear and will probably always remain cobwebbed in mystery. What is almost impossible to nail down is the particular responsibility of the numerous actors in the drama. The events and trends of the year leading up to the GESTAPU must necessarily have a direct bearing on it, which is why they have been described so comprehensively in the preceding pages.

The fact of President Sukarno's illness cannot be doubted. Nor can the effect made by what was popularly believed about his illness on the men in the vortex of power be irrelevant. Their public statements and actions in the days before the *coup d'état* clearly reveal their awareness that time was running out for their own ambitions. The atmosphere of charged expectancy was a fact of common experience. The spate of rumours about plots and counter-plots which preceded GESTAPU provides strong evidence that there was some preparation for the *coup d'état*, and that it was not likely to have been a spontaneous affair.

Of one thing there can be no doubt: the man who actually triggered off the GESTAPU was Colonel Untung. The extent of his responsibility in the original concept and planning of the coup is less certain but, piecing together the statement made at the time by members of the Army High Command, and the assessments of usually knowledgeable Indonesians with access to the confidence of President Sukarno, General Suharto and the officials at Untung's trial, it seems that Untung's part in the *coup d'état* was probably as follows: As Commander of the Palace Guard, Untung had been warned by President Sukarno of rumblings in the Army about the power and ambitions of the PKI. The President feared that the Army might make a pressure move to force him to scrap the NASAKOM government, a concept to which he was as devoted as a Jesuit is to the Holy Trinity. He ordered Untung to be alert for this. Untung has been described as "a muscular moron" – a tough soldier with not much political nous but sufficient cunning and ambition to keep his eye on the main chance. According to his later confession – parts of which came out during his court martial – he discussed his plan for preventing an Army move to force the abolition of NASAKOM with D. N. Aidit, M. H. Lukman, Njono and Njoto – all high-ranking members of the PKI – and with General Omar Dani and Dr Subandrio; never together, but with one or two of them at various times. They collaborated with him and General Omar Dani even suggested that it might become necessary to act quickly if the President died suddenly and left a power vacuum at the top. It was apparently Aidit's scheme, supported by Lukman, to "kidnap" the Army Generals and the Defence Minister General Nasution and, "if necessary", kill them. Dr Subandrio apparently agreed that this was the wisest way to go about it, adding that "the Bung was agreeable" and that it might be necessary to carry out this action even during the President's lifetime if the Army moved against NASAKOM, because Sukarno had said that without NASAKOM there was no meaning to the Revolution or his own life. Thus, the "preventive action" planned by Untung as a part of his police duties was taken several steps further towards a *coup d'état*, which could be carried out either at Sukarno's death or *during his lifetime*.

It is possible that Untung saw in this undertaking the grand opening for his own ambitions and a way out for his own frustration that in a relatively youthful Army he was, at thirty-nine, only a Lieutenant-Colonel, having been superseded by many younger colleagues. His one explanation was that the Gerkang was planned to be contingent on the President's death but was adaptable for earlier operation if the need arose.

To judge from what was disclosed later at the trials of Colonel Untung and of Njoto, the communist leader, both of whom were sentenced to death, the Army has built up a powerful case against the PKI. The PKI, which was also convicted out of court by the general public, has a very different story. Njoto's explanation at his trial was that the PKI had been preparing not a *coup* but a counter-*coup*: they were getting ready to meet an attempt by a conspiratorial body known as the Dewan General – the Council of Generals – to capture power from the President and replace the NASAKOM government with a right-wing military dictatorship.

President Sukarno has yet another version, though very similar to that of the PKI: he has referred publicly to his belief in the Dewan General theory, and is known to have accused General Nasution and the Army Commander General Suharto of guilty knowledge, if not complicity, in a "General's Plot". He concedes that some communist party members as *individuals* were involved in the September 30 Movement.

The Army is convinced that Colonel Untung was only a cat's paw of the PKI and this view seems to be supported by Untung's confession, obtained at the time of his arrest, and by the proceedings at his trial.

The Action Front of the University Scholars (KASI) and the two students' organisations, KAMI and KAPPI, are completely wedded to the belief that Peking was responsible for plotting the GESTAPU together with Dr Subandrio, the PKI and its leader, Aidit.

Many of the details of Aidit's movements on the night of September 30 and the days immediately following will probably never be known. There is, however, enough information provided by statements made by him and his associates, at this time as well as later, to give us a fair picture of his intentions and actions. People who had noticed his quiet exit from the stadium soon after Sukarno's collapse remark that two days previously there had been strong demands from Aidit for the banning of the Islamic

Students' Union. Sukarno had refused and, the story went, there had been an exchange of words which ended in Sukarno slapping Aidit in the face. When Aidit attempted to retaliate, he was removed forcibly by the President's bodyguard. This tale added colour to the conjecture that on the night of the *coup* Aidit left the stadium and made contact with Colonel Untung, who then gave prearranged orders for the *coup* to be carried out. An alternative possibility is that Aidit disappeared to supervise his own plans which had been prepared for the eventuality of the President's death.

There can be little doubt that Aidit had foreknowledge of Colonel Untung's action. This was made clear soon afterwards when the communist commander of the Air Force, General Omar Dani, a close associate of Aidit and Dr Subandrio, publicly supported the *coup d'état*, and when several members of the PKI, including the women's wing, showed that they were privy to it and also played an active part in the events of that night.

According to the Djakarta correspondent of the *Asahi Evening News* of Tokyo, Aidit later made a fifty page confession to the KOSTRAD (Strategic Command). This is his report – a world scoop – of the main points of this document:

"I was the one with the highest responsibility for the September 30 incident and was supported by other PKI officials and officials of the people's organisations under the PKI.

"Dissatisfaction with the existing system was the basic beginning of the idea for this *coup*. If a people's united front government could be established under the leadership of the PKI, the state could get back on its feet, the people's standard of living would improve and a fair society in which there would be no gap between the rich and the poor could be established.

"If the *coup d'état* had succeeded, my policy was to establish closer economic relations with Communist China.

"The PKI originally had set 1970 as its target year but details of this plan leaked out so that relations with the army became unstable. Consequently, the original plan was changed to carry out a *coup* as soon as possible.

"I drafted a plan to be carried out May 1, 1965, but Lukman, Njoto, Sakilman and Njono – all party officials – opposed the plan. They argued it was dangerous since preparations were not completed and that the plan would undoubtedly fail.

"The discussions with Lieutenant-Colonel Untung and others were held many times after June, 1965.

"From July, 1965, action corps of the Pemuda Rakjat, the People's Youth Front, and the Gerwani, the Indonesian women's movement, were gathered at Halim Air Base on the outskirts of Djakarta and were trained in the use of heavy and light weapons. Preparations were pushed.

"When returning from Algeria in early August, I stopped in Peking and discussed the health of President Sukarno with the Communist Chinese leaders.

"As soon as I returned to Djakarta in the middle of the same month, a secret meeting was held. The execution of the *coup d'état* was discussed with Lukman, Njoto, Brigadier-General Supardjo and Lieutenant-Colonel Untung.

"Since we had information that the Army, under orders from Army Minister Yani, would search the Communist Party and related organisations on suspicion of illegal possession of weapons, the situation was such that we could not help but speed up the execution of the *coup d'état*.

"It was on September 25 that we chose the 30th as the date of the *coup*.

"There were proposals that the *coup d'état* be carried

out October 5, Army Day, but the date was moved up because details of our *coup d'état* plan were beginning to leak out.

Sukarno's Refusal

"I ordered Second Vice-Chairman Njoto to Sumatra because I believed that he would be able to persuade the people of Sumatra to our way of thinking.

"Lieutenant-Colonel Untung was made chairman of the Revolutionary Council only as a temporary measure. I did not name myself the man with the highest responsibility for the incident, except within the PKI, because of considerations concerning the possibility of success of the *coup d'état.*

"We asked President Sukarno to sign the bill establishing the Revolutionary Council and to broadcast this to the whole nation, but he refused.

"The position of the President was to have been maintained even after the *coup d'état* had succeeded, but we intended to criticise and revise his policies gradually.

"As for the five basic principles of Indonesia's political philosophy – religion, nationalism, humanism, democracy and socialism – we planned to gradually reduce their use and eventually make them nothing more than figureheads.

"Also, after the success of the *coup d'état* we intended to form a 'fifth military force' apart from the existing four military forces centred around the People's Youth Front, BTI (Farmer's Front), SOBSI (Central Indonesian Federation of Labour Unions) and the other organisations under the PKI.

"The *coup d'état* failed because it was premature and also because there were not a few – even among the top PKI officials – who were opposed. I recognise this fact.

"In the secret meeting of the PKI Central Committee, the *coup d'état* was originally scheduled for 1970.

"The second reason for the failure was the lack of

support of Communist China and international communism on which we had placed hopes.

PKI infiltration

"PKI power had infiltrated 25 per cent of the Indonesian Army, but they did not act as we had expected them to. This was because the anti-communist group within the army was too strong and because the army carried out mop-up operations so speedily.

"I was in Djakarta from September 30 to October 1, leading the *coup* try. At Halim Air Base, I informed President Sukarno of the existence of the council of generals and of the *coup d'état* plan, but he apparently did not believe me.

"Together with others, I showed him the bill for establishment of the Revolutionary Council and asked him to approve it, but the President refused.

"During this time, Army Minister Yani and five other generals were killed by armed members of our side in the vicinity of the air base.

"As a result of the Djakarta Central Broadcasting Station having been taken away from us by forces commanded by Major-General Suharto (now Lieutenant-General and Army Minister as well as Army Commander), an emergency meeting was held.

"The meeting was attended by Lieutenant-Colonel Untung, Brigadier-General Supardjo, PKI 1st Secretary Lukman and Political Bureau member Njono.

"However, we recognised that the *coup d'état* in Djakarta had failed. I decided to fly to Central Java, establish a revolutionary council there and work to maintain and revive power.

"I left Halim Air Base at 1.30 a.m. on October 2 by plane and arrived at Djogjakarta Base at 3 a.m. I told the commander of the air base, 'Since the situation in Djakarta is unstable, there is a possibility that President

Sukarno will take refuge in Djogjakarta, so I am to make a prior check.'

"On October 2, I went from Djogjakarta to Semarang and from Semarang to Solo. At all these places, I instructed the government officials and army officers who were pro-PKI to establish revolutionary councils. I intended to have the council in Solo become the nucleus for revolutionary councils in Central Java.

"At 8.30 a.m. on October 3, I met the commander of the Solo Air Base and asked that he provide me with a plane to fly to Djakarta or Bali Island, but he refused.

Finally Captured

"As a result, I worked on the plan to collect communist power in Central Java. I inspected the various areas around Solo and provided leadership until about October 21. Up to this time I was comparatively safe.

"The uprising in Solo, decided as the central point in Central Java, was scheduled for October 23, and orders were sent out to all areas. Orders were issued to the PKI cells to cut down the trees alongside the roads leading into Surakarta, at 12.01 a.m., on October 23, to form barricades, carry out general strikes in the government offices, government railways and government firms and arrest the leaders of rightist groups.

"However, early on the morning of October 23 the RPKAD (paratroopers) and KOSTRAD (strategic corps) of the Army advanced into Solo and grabbed power so that the uprising plan failed."

Another account of what happened, unearthed by certain Indonesian journalists – who shall be nameless here in their own interest – but which was never printed in the Indonesian press (which, at that time, dared not publish anything not released by the Army) goes as follows.

Colonel Untung had pressed the button for the *coup d'état* planned to take place in the event of the President's death, and went ahead with his prearranged motions of taking control until he could hand over the reins of authority to Dr Subandrio as the civil leader and to General Omar Dani, head of the Air Force, as the leader of the military arm. His own future as a power in the land had been assured. With the PKI supporting the rebellion, with promises of active assistance from army units in Central and East Java, with assured support from the leadership of the KKO (marines) and the police, and with some possible support from Army units there was a chance of his being able to take and retain power in the inevitable confusion caused by the removal of the top generals commanding the Army.

Untung went blazing ahead, preparing the ground for the take-over. On the night of September 30 Tchakrabirawa troops supported by armed youths of the Pemuda Front took control of Radio Djakarta. A communiqué was prepared for broadcasting at the earliest hour. A Pemuda Front communist group known as The Information Section of the September 30 Movement was entrusted with the task of broadcasting the communiqué repeatedly over Radio Republic Indonesia. The tortured wording of Untung's first communiqué exposes the fears of his fellow conspirators and offers some clues to their identity:

COMMUNIQUE OF "30 SEPTEMBER MOVEMENT".

"Djakarta, October 1. Antara: "The 'Movement of 30 September' issued a communiqué explaining latest developments taking place in the country.

"The statement said that on Thursday, September 30, 1965, a military movement among the Army took place in Djakarta, the capital of the Republic of Indonesia, which was aided by other units of the other branches of the Armed Forces.

"The 'September 30 Movement' which was headed by Lieutenant-Colonel Untung, Commandant of the Tchakrabirawa Battalion, security guards of President Sukarno, was directed against generals who were members of what was called 'Council of Generals', the communiqué said.

"A number of generals had been arrested and important communications means and some other vital installations put under control of the 'September 30 Movement', while President Sukarno was safe under the protection of 'September 30 Movement'. Also a number of popular leaders who would have been the objective of the Council of Generals had been placed under the protection of the 'September 30 Movement', the statement announced. The announcement said that the 'Council of Generals' was a subversive movement sponsored by the Central Intelligence Agency (CIA) which was very active lately particularly so when President Sukarno was gravely ill during the first week of last August.

"Their hope that President Sukarno would die because of his illness was belied. In this connection, to achieve their designs, the 'Council of Generals' had organized a 'show of force' on Armed Forces Day, this October 5 by deploying troops from East Java, Central Java and West Java to here. With the big concentration of military troops in Djakarta, the 'Council of Generals' had planned a military *coup d'état* before October 5, 1965. To prevent this counter-revolutionary *coup*, Lieutenant-Colonel Untung was forced to organise the 'September 30 Movement' which met with complete success.

"According to information from Lieutenant-Colonel Untung, Commandant of the September 30 Movement, the movement was solely a movement within the Army and directed against the 'Council of Generals' which had harmed the good name of the Army and had bad intentions against the Republic of Indonesia and President Sukarno. Lieutenant-Colonel Untung, personally considered the movement as imperative as a member of the Tchakrabirawa Regiment which had the task to protect the safety of the President of the Republic of Indonesia.

"The Commandant of the September 30 Movement also said that steps already taken in Djakarta against the 'Council of Generals' would be followed with similar action throughout Indonesia and directed against the agents and henchmen as well as sympathisers of the 'Council of Generals' in the regions. The leaders of the September 30 Movement also said that as follow-up measures, an 'Indonesian Revolutionary Council' will be formed in the centre, with provincial revolutionary councils in the provinces, regional revolutionary and *ketjamatan* and village revolutionary councils in the rural areas.

"The members of these revolutionary councils will be civilians and military officers who unreservedly support the 'September 30 Movement'. Political parties and popular organisations, newspapers, magazines and the like would be permitted to carry on their activities provided that within a certain time limit to be determined later, stated their loyalty to the Indonesian Revolutionary Council.

"The Indonesian Revolutionary Council, which will be formed by the 'September 30 Movement', would consistently carry out the *Pantja Azimat* (five talismans) of the Revolution, the decisions adopted by the Provisional People's Consultative Assembly (MPRS), the Gotong Royong House of Representatives and the Supreme Advisory Council (DPA), the Commandant of the 'September 30 Movement' said.

"The Indonesian Revolutionary Council would not change Indonesia's foreign policy, which was independent and active against neocolonialism, imperialism and colonialism in the interest of preserving peace in South-east Asia and the world. Policies in regard to the holding of the second Afro-Asian Conference in Algiers, the Conference of New Emerging Forces and confrontation against 'Malaysia' would not be altered. The Conference against foreign military bases (KIAPMA) and other international activities which had been decided for holding in Indonesia would be carried on as planned.

"Lieutenant-Colonel Untung as Commandant of the September 30 Movement also appealed to the whole Indonesian people to continue preserving vigilance and assist the September 30 Movement without reserve to safeguard the Republic of Indonesia from the bad designs of the 'Council of Generals' and its tools, and carry out the Message of Suffering of the People in the true sense of the word.

"To officers, non-commissioned officers and ranks of the Army throughout the country, Commandant Lieutenant-Colonel Untung appealed for firm determination and action to destroy all influences of the 'Council of Generals' and its agents and tools within the Army. The generals and officers who were lusting for power, who ignored the poor fate of their men, and live in luxury and a spendrift life at their expense and humiliate women and also waste government funds must be kicked out from the Army and given equal sentence.

"The Army was not the property of the generals but the property of all the officers of the Army who are loyal to the aspirations and goals of the August 1945 Revolution. To all units of forces which did not belong to the Army Lieutenant-Colonel Untung expressed high gratitude for their assistance to the steps taken to cleanse the Army, and hoped that similar action would be taken within the ranks of these forces concerned against the sympathisers and agents of the 'Council of Generals'.

"Soon Commandant Lt. Colonel Untung would issue the First Decree on the Indonesian Revolutionary Council which would be followed by other decrees.

"The communiqué was issued in Djakarta, September 30, 1965, by the Information Section of the September 30 Movement.

"The communiqué was repeatedly broadcast by RRI, Djakarta today from 8.00 a.m."

The complicity of Dr Subandrio in the composition of this text is regarded by the Indonesian journalists referred to above as being evident in the apparently interpolatory paragraph concerning Indonesian foreign policy and the importance of the Algiers Conference of Afro-Asian Nations, and the Conference Against Foreign Bases, both of which loomed large in the mind of Subandrio but not in Untung's. The statement that Commandant Lieutenant-Colonel Untung was to issue the First Decree of the Indonesian Revolutionary Council provided the first solid proof that Untung believed that the President was dead, or that his removal from effective power was an essential part of the plan.

Further substantial evidence of this was soon forthcoming. On October 1 another communiqué was issued by the Information Section of the Indonesian Revolutionary Council:

NAMES OF MEMBERS OF
"INDONESIAN REVOLUTIONARY COUNCIL".
"Djakarta, October 1. Antara: The Information Section of the September 30 Movement this afternoon announced the formation of an 'Indonesian Revolutionary Council.'
1. Lieutenant Colonel Untung – Council Chairman
2. Brigadier General Supardjo – Council Vice Chairman
3. Air Lieutenant Colonel Heru – Vice Chairman
4. Police Chief Commissioner Anwar – Vice Chairman and members:
"Vice Admiral Omar Dani, Police Inspector General Sutjipto Judodihardjo, Vice Admiral Martadinata, Dr Subandrio, 10. Dr J. Leimena, 11. Surachman (nationalist), Fatah Jasin (religious), K. H. Siradjuddin Abbas (religious), Tjugito (Communist), Arudji Kartawinata, Siauw Giok Tjan, Sumarno SH, Hartono (Major

Djenderal KKO), Sukarto (Police Brig. Gen.), Zaini Mansjur (Front Pemuda Pusat), Jahja SH (Front Pemuda), Sukatno (Front Pemuda), Bambang Kusnohadi (PPMI), A. Rachman (Front Nasional), Hardojo (Student), Basuki Rachmat (Major General), Ryacudu (Brig. Gen.), Solichin (Brig. Gen.), Amir Machmud (Brig. Gen.), Andi Rivai (Brig. Gen.), Sujono (Air Major), Leo Wattimena (Air Komodor), Nj. Utami Suryadarma, A. Latif (Kolonel), Umar Wirahadikusuma (Maj. Gen.), Mrs Supeni, Mrs Mahmudah Mwardi, Mrs Suharti Suwarto, Fattah (Colonel), Suherman (Colonel), Colonel Sjamsu Sutjipto (Navy Col.), Suhardi (journalist), Drs Sumarsono, Djunta Suardi, Karim DP (journalist).

"The Chairman and Vice Chairman of the Council are members of the Indonesian Revolutionary Council, and represent the Council in its daily task.

"It was announced that all members of the civil group sitting in the Revolutionary Council received the rank of Lt. Col. All others above the rank of Lt. Colonel were demoted to the same rank of Lt. Colonel.

"Meanwhile all officers and non-commissioned officers of the Armed Forces were raised in rank one grade above of that which they held prior to September 30, 1965. While non-commissioned officers and troops who had taken part in the clean up of September 30 were promoted two ranks.

"All officers of higher rank than Lt. Colonel were requested to declare their loyalty to the Revolutionary Council after which they were entitled to hold the rank of Lt. Colonel."

There was a major omission from the list of members of the Revolutionary Council: the name of President Sukarno. In later communiqués Untung tried to cover up this omission by explaining that the President who was under the "protection" of the September 30 Movement was of course head of the Council in his capacity as President. On October 1 Antara reported:

PRESIDENT SUKARNO CONTINUES TO HEAD STATE

"The Commander of Tchakrabirawa Regiment, announced this afternoon that President/Great Leader of the Revolution Bung Karno was in good health and continued to hold the helm of the state.

"The announcement was made through RRI, Djakarta, and before newsmen by Lieutenant-Colonel M. Santoso, chief of staff of the Tchakrabirawa Regiment, at the Regiment's headquarters this morning.

"The announcement said: 'To avoid wrong interpretations and misreporting, we announce that President/Great Leader of the Revolution Bung Karno is in good health and that he continues to head the State'."

But, by that time many other events had overtaken Colonel Untung's plans and ambitions. From Madiun came the first signal from the Air Force commander General Omar Dani who was to become the effective power according to the plans of the September 30 Gerkang. The signal was dated Friday, October 1, 1965 at 9.30 a.m.

ORDER OF THE DAY

1. The Movement of September 30th has gone into action to save the Revolution and the Great Leader of the Revolution from CIA's subversion.

For this reason an epuration took place in the Army against foreign subversive elements who endangered the Indonesian Revolutions.

2. After this epuration, the subversive elements of foreign origin will not remain inactive and will most probably intensify their anti-revolutionary activities.

3. As a tool of the Revolution, the Air Force will always support any revolutionary progressive movement.

Inversely the Air Force will attack anything endangering the Indonesian Revolution.

4. With this order of the day, I order to all members of the Air Force to be on alert against provocations and efforts made to undermine the Revolution and to strengthen their vigilance towards all activities of foreign as well as of internal origin.

Air Force General Omar Dani,
Minister/Commander of the Air Force.

Chapter X

SUKARNO AT HALIM

Where did Sukarno go after the meeting in the stadium? How did he spend those crucial hours between midnight and dawn when the *Gerkang* was in full swing and the generals were being murdered? For days many conjectures were floating around Djakarta. The least plausible among them was that he was "under doctors' orders" and confined to his bed at Merdeka Palace. Some said he was in the house of one of the "Palace Millionaires", the group of rupiah multi-millionaires who haunted the Palace and provided Sukarno with the funds he needed to keep up his extravagant style in return for special trading and foreign exchange permits. His Japanese wife later told the press that he had spent the night with her. The version accepted at that time by the most hard-nosed journalists in Indonesia was that he was placed "under protective custody" at the Palace by Untung who was trying, vainly, to persuade him to sign a document approving of the Gerkang and the capture of the generals.

According to this story Untung, flabbergasted that the President had made such a swift recovery, tried to turn this circumstance to serve his purpose by persuading Sukarno to go along with – and indeed head – an action that had been started in the belief that he was dead or dying. Sukarno protested that he could not sign any document until he could "feel the pulse of the people" and asked for time to "consult the masses". Untung then held up the President at the point of his revolver and conveyed him by jeep to Halim Air Base. His intention, according to this version of events, was to hand Sukarno over to General Omar Dani's "safekeeping". When Untung arrived with his explosive passenger, the soldiers at Halim recognised the President and crowded round the jeep. Sukarno promptly began making a speech. In the general confusion, Untung disappeared and went back to Djakarta, and from Djakarta to the provinces where he hid himself away for several days before he was caught and brought back to be tried for armed conspiracy against the President and the people of the Republic of Indonesia.

Whatever the truth of this version of the story, one significant fact is clearly established. President Sukarno was at Halim air base at dawn on October 1. This caused widespread confusion and suspicion about his own relationship to the *Gestapu* movement – and may well be one of the crucial clues to unravelling the mysteries of that night. Denis Warner, writing in *The Reporter* on November 19, implies that the President had gone to Halim in order to join forces with Omar Dani and D. N. Aidit. Warner, reporting a visit from Dr Johannes Leimena, the Second Deputy Premier, says:

"Later in the day, with great courage, Johannes Leimena, Second Deputy Premier, having discovered Sukarno's whereabouts, went to Halim air base. He persuaded the President that the *coup* was broken and that under no circumstances should he accompany Aidit and Omar Dani, who were preparing to fly to Central Java and urging Sukarno to go with them. Sukarno accepted Leimena's advice and went instead to his Palace in Bogor, thirty-three miles south of Djakarta."

A statement issued by President Sukarno and broadcast at 6 a.m. on October 4 seems to confirm Warner's report:

"I went to the Halim Perdanakusuma Air Force base on the morning of October 1 of my own free will because I considered it was the best place for me to have a plane which could take me to another place in case of unpredictable events."

Warner's comment on this was: "Sukarno's own version is that because of the suspicious presence of troops, he left the palace under escort at 6 a.m. on October 1 and went to the Halim air base, where he keeps the Presidential jet. The air base is only fifteen miles from Djakarta . . . It took an explained but expedient three and a half hours to make the journey."

Another version suggests that he had arrived at the air base earlier and was there at the same time that the generals were brought in and murdered. This is the Army version and, because the tide was turning swiftly in favour of the Army which, overnight had become the "good guys", it was also a popular version. It insinuated that the President had been in the conspiracy to murder the generals and that Untung had carried out his *coup d'état* with the knowledge and active cooperation of the President. In other words, it was a *coup d'état* against the Army and the right wing carried out by the President, Aidit, Dr Subandrio and General Omar Dani.

The Washington correspondent of *The Times*, London, later provided confirmation for this point of view:

U.S. CLAIMS SUKARNO WAS INVOLVED IN COUP

Washington, Oct 13. Intelligence sources here claim that there is incontrovertible evidence that President Sukarno was involved in the attempted *coup* of September 30 and that the objective of the President and the Communist Party was the elimination of the military command. If such evidence exists, it has not been made available, but confessions have been quoted to support the charge against the Communist Party.

They have it that the party mobilised several armed bands on September 28 whose leaders cooperated with

Colonel Untung in the assassination of six senior military commanders. Their exact whereabouts were known, and the seventh, General Nasution, the Defence Minister, was fortunate to survive, although wounded.

Previously, the evidence of communist complicity was rather meagre, and the amateurishness of the attempt hardly made it more persuasive. The State Department still remains unconvinced, and the fresh but secret evidence appears to have come from the Central Intelligence Agency. It is conceded, however, that the circumstances could have led President Sukarno to side with the communists.

What now concerns the State Department is the possible consequences. The assumption is that the military will not remove President Sukarno, who is still very much a political force. The hope is that the Communist Party will be declared illegal, but there is no general expectation that it will be realised.

The Times, London, Oct. 14, 1965.

The truth probably lies somewhere between these varying versions. There can be no doubt that the President was concerned about rumours of a Council of Generals plotting to destroy the NASAKOM complex of government that he had set up and held together with great difficulty. There is also no doubt that he gave hope and refuge after the *coup d'état* was foiled to the people who were publicly accused of complicity: Subandrio and Omar Dani were given sanctuary in his palace for weeks when the Army's man-hunt was at its keenest. Other acts of omission, too, strengthen the impression that Sukarno's relationship with the GESTAPU leaders was motivated by something other than judicial impartiality. His reluctance to attend the funeral of the six generals and his failure to offer his condolences to General and Mrs Nasution on the death of their child until nearly three weeks had passed, were widely seen as indications of his personal guilt in the murders.

A clear, logical story may never emerge from this welter of contradictory possibilities. However, having sifted the facts, possibilities and probabilities for ten months, it seems to me that the real explanation may well include salient elements from all these versions. Briefly, there were probably three different plans or "actions" ready and set to go about that time:

(1) The preparations of the Army to counter any attempt by Subandrio and the PKI to make a take-over bid with the military backing of the Air Force in case the President died. This was what Sukarno, Colonel Untung and the PKI referred to as the Dewan General or Council of Generals.

(2) Colonel Untung's preparations, possibly begun in response to the President's warning, against a possible Army plan to bring down the NASAKOM government during or after Sukarno's lifetime and (3) the plans of the PKI to take power if the President died, with military assistance from the Air Force, and to establish a government probably with Dr Subandrio as the nominal civilian head.

Any plans the Army had, went awry that night when the generals were butchered. Whether preparations for the manoeuvres of October 5 had sinister significance or not, they certainly helped General Nasution and General Suharto to crush the Untung *coup d'état* as easily as an egg-shell. The other two "actions" on the Left very probably became intertwined as the fear of the Army plans for October 5 rose to a peak during the preceding days and almost certainly became unified, albeit raggedly, when the news of President Sukarno's collapse was taken as the signal that he was dying.

This reading ties up almost all the loose ends: it explains why the Revolutionary Council left Sukarno out of their list; why Sukarno did not share the public anger at the murder of the generals; why he might have considered throwing in his lot with Dani and Aidit on October 1; why he made the gratuitous statement about going to Halim of his own free will; why he refused to ban the PKI when the Army pleaded and later demanded it; why he protected Subandrio through the most precarious days of his effective power. And it also explains his fears – confirmed by later events – that the Army would deflect the Leftward march of the Indonesian Revolution. His sneering public statement on November 7 that "Mr Marshall Green, the United States Ambassador, has told diplomats that the US is jubilant over the unsuccessful pro-communist coup of October 1" makes that abundantly clear.

Chapter XI

ENTER NASUTION, SUHARTO

The first part of the *coup d'état* produced quite a bag but it was not complete. The murder squads had missed out two victims – a mistake which proved to be crucial. They failed to get two of the most important of the men marked for butchering: General Nasution and General Suharto.

When the Tchakrabirawa detail came to Nasution's house in Djalan Tenku Umar, two hours before dawn, the armed guard at the gate became suspicious and refused to let them in. A gun battle ensued and two of the guards were killed. The detail then went into the house to go through the routine of delivering a verbal summons from the President and taking Nasution away, alive or dead. Aroused from his sleep by the shooting, Lieutenant Tendean, one of Nasution's aides, alerted the General and his family. There are many divergent stories about what followed, the most convincing of which is that which Mrs Nasution told her friends. She said that Lieutenant Tendean, a man with the same build and appearance as Nasution, put on his chief's uniform-jacket and peaked cap and went out to greet the visitors "to give Nasution time to get away". The detail commander said: "General Nasution?" Tendean replied with a curt "Yes. What is it?" He was forcibly carried to the waiting truck to be taken to Halim. Well on the way to Halim, one of the men became suspicious and turned his flashlight beam on their captive. Lieutenant Tendean was promptly killed and the gang returned to Djalan Tenku Umar.

Meanwhile Mrs Nasution had pleaded with her husband to leave the house and seek refuge elsewhere, but he was determined to stay and fight it out. When the murder squad returned, Mrs Nasution all but pushed him out of a window at the back of the house. She then went to the protection of her five-year-old daughter. She locked the child's bedroom door and tried to compose herself. Within a few minutes the lock of the bedroom was shattered by a bullet, the door flew open and some men walked in shooting. The child was shot five times – possibly mistaken for the General in the dim light of predawn. Mrs Nasution picked up the wounded child and rushed into the street, begging for a lift to the hospital. When she reached the hospital the child was still alive and the surgeons got to work on her. Mrs Nasution then got in touch with the Police and the Army, and alerted them about the Tchakarabirawa being on the rampage. Nasution's child died shortly after. He himself managed to climb over the heavily barbed-wired garden wall and down into his neighbour's compound, badly injuring his leg in the process. He then thumbed a ride and reached Army headquarters within an hour of the attack.

There Major-General Suharto was waiting. He was aware that a *coup d'état* was taking place and that the Army generals had been kidnapped, but he had no political directions to give to his men. The President was missing, the generals had been captured and there was no one to whom he could turn until Nasution arrived. Suharto later said that he had "never been happier to see any man, particularly Nasution".

The way in which Suharto himself escaped assassination is one of those strange stories with which Indonesia abounds: a tale of mysticism, prophecy and faith. It is not at all necessary to believe in any of these mysteries to appreciate the significance of the story. It is only necessary to realise that General Suharto himself believes that his *dukun*, or guru, has prophetic powers and that he follows this man's guidance which, according to him, is given by Suharto's *devas* or guardian angels.

On September 25 the *dukun* told General Suharto that he should not return to his house before 2 a.m. on the night of September 30 or, rather, on the morning of October 1.* Suharto was advised to spend the night hours "worshipping God at a place where the waters meet". When he came off duty that evening he therefore went to the river mouth and sailed out to where the sea and the river waters meet, and spent four or five hours doing his *zikkir*, praising God, and contemplating His greatness and uniqueness. When he approached his home it was long after 2 o'clock. But he noticed some jeeps and lorries standing outside his house, and a great deal of unusual activity. He turned his car round and went directly to Army Headquarters and there received the information that the President was gravely ill and that there was some sort of political crisis on. He tried to call his superiors, General Yani, General Suprapto and General Harjono, but was unable to get through. It was about 4 a.m. when the rumours of the shooting of General Yani and the kidnapping of the other Generals reached him. He was, as he said later, very calm, knowing that his spiritual guardians who had saved him from capture and possible murder would send him guidance.

Guidance came in the person of General Nasution. As Defence Minister, Nasution was in a position to give the Army political direction in the absence of the President, whose whereabouts was not known. Nasution and Suharto at Army headquarters began taking counter-action against the *coup d'état*. Swift action was taken against the new guards at Radio Djakarta. The Radio Station was soon captured and the Army took commanding positions on the trunk routes at vantage points round the capital. While they were directing these operations a call came through from Halim

*The fact that all these events took place between 9 p.m. of September 30 and the early hours of October 1 has created some confusion in the slogans devised for them. GESTAPU was invented for September 30. Those who are more prosaic prefer the less imaginative *Ger*kang *Ok*tober abbreviated into GESTOK.

Air Base informing them of the President's presence there. Suharto safe-conducted the President to Bogor, thirty miles away. With the President safely ensconced in his Palace with a guard of Paratroop Commandos, with General Nasution and General Suharto directing operations at Army headquarters and with the tight control they had taken of the city's defences and the radio station, the *coup d'état* became a pathetic failure.

As soon as it was known that the GESTAPU had been smashed in Djakarta there was a general scramble among all the left wing forces to dissociate themselves from it. October 2 was their great day for hand-washing. General Omar Dani issued his second communiqué on behalf of the Air Force:

SECOND STATEMENT OF THE AIR FORCE

1. The Air Force has no contact with the "Movement of September 30th".
2. The Air Force agrees with any epuration made in all the organisations of the Revolution along the line defined by the Great Leader of the Revolution.
3. The Air Force does not interfere in the internal affairs of the other arms.
4. The Air Force does not know anything of the existence of a "Revolutionary Council" or of the composition of the list of its members.

Air Force military base Halim Perdana Kasuma,
Oct 2, 1965.
Minister/Commander of the Air Force
Omar Dani, Air Force General.

This was the man who, twenty-four hours earlier had said: "The Movement of September 30 has gone into action to save the Revolution and the Great Leader of the Revolution from CIA's subversion."

Equally quick off the mark were the PWI leaders, the communists in the journalists' association which had churned out managed news for the public ever since the press was captured. After a night of celebration following their promotion to the Revolutionary Council they issued a statement denying any knowledge of Untung's intentions:

> PWI STATEMENT
> Djakarta, Oct 2 (Antara): In connection with the inclusion of the names of General Chairman of the Indonesian Journalists' Association (PWI) A. Karim DP and Head of PWI Juridical Section Soehardi in the "Revolutionary Council", the Central Board of PWI emphasised that it had been done without prior consultation with PWI Central Board.
>
> PWI Central Board in this connection emphasised that it fully stood behind the Great Leader of the Revolution/Supreme Commander of the Armed Forces Bung Karno in his policy to accomplish the Indonesian Revolution.

This statement was dated October 1 but was, apparently, issued in the early hours of October 2 when the text of Dani's second communiqué had reached the Antara agency office. The Left wing of the PNI, the Nationalist Party which was founded by Sukarno himself, also rushed in with their disclaimer: It was printed in the PNI newspaper *Suluh Indonesia:*

> P.N.I. CENTRAL BOARD KNOWS NOTHING
> Djkarta, Oct 2 (Sulindo): "In connection with the inclusion of the names of members of the P.N.I. (Indonesian Nationalist Party) in the list of members of the "Revolutionary Council", the Central Board of the P.N.I., in a press statement last night asserted that the Board knows nothing about and bears no responsibility for the inclusion of those names.
>
> In addition, the members of the P.N.I. whose names were used by the "Revolutionary Council", namely

> Surachman, Zaini Mansjur, Bambang Kusnohadi, Supeni, Sumarno S.H. and A. Karim D.P., declare that they know nothing about and bear no responsibility for the using of their names.
>
> This is the press statement issued by the Central Board of the P.N.I. last night.

There were three reasons for these swift turnabouts. First, the commonsense motive of getting out from under a crumbling house; second, the fear that General Nasution and the Army would wreak immediate vengeance on those held responsible for the assassination of the generals; and third, the news that Sukarno had thrown his massive weight on the side of the Army. This, as it turned out, was entirely expedient and temporary, but who was to know it at that time?

At midnight on October 2, following a five hours conference with General Suharto at Bogor Palace, President Sukarno confirmed the fears of the Left when he issued an official statement that he was physically well and was still the leader of the nation. He announced that he, as Commander-in-Chief, had assumed full control of the Army and that he had appointed General Suharto to be responsible for "restoring peace".

People in Djakarta continue to speculate what would have happened had Sukarno thrown in his lot at that time with the Left and not with the Army. There are those who even feel that it was Sukarno who caused the rout of the PKI by not giving Omar Dani the chance of using the military might of the Air Force and the deeply communist-penetrated KKO marines against Nasution and Suharto when the army had lost its topmost leaders. In point of fact, whether Sukarno was sympathetic to the action against the generals or not, he had no alternative but to appoint Suharto to "get to the bottom of the Gerkang" because public feelings had been so deeply stirred against Untung by the fate of the generals. When their bodies were discovered on October 4, any man who condoned the butchery publicly would almost certainly have been lynched.

It was apparently on Mrs Djamilah's evidence (quoted on page 80) that the Army began an intensive search of the air base and its surroundings. Eventually they came to Crocodile Well, a hole 36 metres deep and one metre wide into which the bodies of the six generals and General Pandjaitan's dead bodyguard had been dumped. When they were exhumed, the horror was intensified. The Gerwani – the PKI women – had added an Ian Fleming touch to their work. The genitals of some of the men had been cut off and were found stuffed into their mouths. The reason for the colour of the blindfolds described by Mrs Djamilah was that they were drenched in blood. The victims' captors had gouged out their eyes before delivering them up to the Gerwani for their special attention.

Rumours of these brutalities had been abroad for some days when the bodies were recovered. The Army made gruesome but enormously successful capital out of their find. Photographs of the mutilated bodies, with descriptions of what had taken place, were printed in the newspapers. There were insets of the instrument employed as an eye-gouger – a piece of bent barrel-hoop crudely shaped to fit the murderer's grip and the victim's eye. The bloody clothes were put on display. And, to top it all, the pictures were shown on television repeatedly.

Almost immediately the Army's campaign against the PKI and its affiliates became a people's movement. The masses who had up to now been passive witnesses to the PKI's efforts to capture power in Indonesia, turned on the communists with a fierce heat which I have seen only once before in my experience as a reporter: that was in Kerala, South India, when the public launched a massive and successful protest against the Communist government in power. A kind of national expiation seemed to be taking place. People seemed to be asking themselves: "How can we Indonesians do such things, especially to our own people? Surely there must be some foreign influence involved?"

The mood of the times was such that the dead generals, Nasution and Suharto were transformed into enormously heroic figures, dwarfing all lesser beings and almost reaching the stature of Bung Karno. Nasution, Suharto and the Army now appeared to the public as the giants who had rescued their demi-god Sukarno from the machinations of the GESTAPU conspirators and had restored the sacred Indonesian Revolution after the attempt to pervert it by *coup d'état*. The history of those dramatic days was to be clearly read on the walls of Djakarta. First the pre-*coup* slogans were hidden under huge red daubs screaming, HIDUP UNTUNG (Long live Untung) – GANJANG ABRI (crush the armed forces) – GANJANG CIA – HIDUP CONSIL REVOLUSI. Then these new slogans welcoming the Revolutionary Council were almost obscured in their turn by a bold new set of scribblings, quite different from those which had decorated the walls for so many years: HIDUP ABRI – HIDUP NASUTION – HIDUP SUHARTO. And among these the most euphonious and telling was GANTUNG UNTUNG (hang Untung).

Within a week, particularly after the discovery of the mutilated bodies, the slogan campaign had been taken deep into the territory of the very people who had invented this form of warfare. Every inch of wall space and road space was covered with denunciations of the GESTAPU and its suspected participants. And for the first time D.N. Aidit was denounced by the slogan scribblers: AIDIT GANTUNG (hang Aidit) – BUBARKAN PKI (ban the PKI) – GANJANG PKI – AIDIT PAHLAWAN GESTAPU (Aidit is the champion of the Gestapu) – AIDIT SALIP (crucify Aidit).

When the full story of the mutilation of the generals came out the slogans began raving against the Women's wing of the PKI: GERWANI TJABOL (the Gerwani are whores) – GANTUNG GERWANI – GANJANG GERWANI.

At this stage of the slogan war the Muslim parties evidently joined in. The denunciations took a crusading tone: PKI ANTI-TUHAN (The PKI is anti-God) – AIDIT SETEN (Aidit is Satan).

And the first charges of complicity were made against the Chinese residents in Indonesia and against Peking: GANJANG BEPARKI (crush the party of the Chinese residents) – PEKING KASIF PKI (Peking is the treasurer of the PKI).

Although the uprising was quelled in the capital within twelve hours, in Central and East Java, where the PKI had considerable rural support and had infiltrated deep into military units, the fighting continued. For two days Djakarta was agog with rumours that battalions of the Diponegoro Division under the command of Colonel Suharman was marching on the city. The tanks of the RPKAD, the ground-based paratroop commandos attached to the Western-based regiments of the Siliwangi Division, were deployed round the city and formed themselves into steel fortresses at strategic points such as the Djakarta bypass, Kemajoran airport and Tandjung Priok. The expected attack never materialised. But in the hills of Central Java and around Madiun, communist troops in the armed forces fought a series of confused battles against the army units deployed by General Suharto. Many of the rebel troops were from the Diponeegoro Division in which Untung had commanded a battalion before he was posted to head the elite Tchakrabirawa Regiment. The absence of reliable news from these remote districts left the field open to wild rumour, which rampaged freely, blowing up the rebellion into enormously exaggerated proportions. As it happened, the rebels were beaten before they had started. The fact that Sukarno and Omar Dani had already declared themselves against the Gerkang of September 30 had taken the guts out of their fight. And General Suharto was a superb fighter in the field, and General Nasution a master of the art of guerilla warfare in Indonesian conditions.*

General Ibrahim Adjie, commanding the Siliwangi Division, issued a clear ultimatum to the rebel forces: "There is a limit to the Army's patience. If you do not stop your resistance, the strongest measures will be taken. Any action aimed at obstructing the Presidential prerogative constitutes an act against the Revolution. The trust put by the President in appointing Major-General Suharto to carry out the task of restoring law and order will be carried out by the Army until its conclusion."

The remnants of the Tchakrabirawa forces still fighting in the outskirts of Djakarta were given seventy-two hours in which to capitulate. Their raggle-taggle action dwindled down to nothing before that deadline. In the hills the guerillas, cut away from these developments in the capital, dragged on their resistance for a few weeks. Fierce fighting went on at Klaten, after the rebels had been ousted from Djokjakarta on October 5. But by October 13 the Army was in full control of East Java. Central Java was still untidy but the rebel cause was hopeless now that a substantial segment of the public had turned against the September 30 Movement. But General Suharto was compelled to declare a "State of War" in Central Java since the rebels, in desperation, were ransacking the countryside for supplies of food.

There were fears that the situation around Djogjakarta might blow up into a civil war, but these proved to be unfounded because the rebels had now two enemies to fight! – the Army and the people, who had turned on anyone suspected of involvement in the *Gerkang*. Reports of the fate of the generals had percolated into these areas and mass vengeance was being taken against PKI members and their affiliates. The rebels' guerilla activities were regarded

*General Nasution's book on guerilla tactics is widely regarded as a classic.

as a sustained campaign of murder against the common people. Antara reported that the PKI had slaughtered nearly two hundred Muslims in Central Java and that the bodies of sixty-eight civilians killed by poisoning had been found in a mass grave near Madiun. These stories of atrocities inevitably led to massive popular reprisals and the Army's problems were now complicated by the additional duty of keeping the civilian population quiet.

While these brutalities were going on in the hills, civilian life in Djakarta was being restored to a fair state of equilibrium. In the intervening days Nasution and Suharto had displayed greater capacities as tacticians than anyone had previously credited them with. The Army proved that its Intelligence sources were as good as, possibly better than, those of the PKI or Dr Subandrio.

Within a few days of smashing the coup, the entire PKI organisation in and around Djakarta was destroyed. This was done by a device so simple in its conception and execution that the Army officers who carried it out still chuckle about it. Army Intelligence knew that the PKI had followed the book in setting up its urban structure. The organisation was composed of cells arranged in what the Army called the Inverted V or the Baseless Triangle pattern. At the bottom of each arm of the V there was a communist cell. Each was directed by a cell leader sitting at the apex but neither of the cells had knowledge of each other's existence except through the leader, thus making it possible for one to continue its activities if the other was discovered and destroyed. It was an admirable arrangement but, as it turned out, there was a catch. The Army picked up 1,006 cell leaders in and around Djakarta in a single swoop in one night. The PKI cells were thrown into complete disarray and could not regroup into a striking force to take counteraction. This pattern of operations was repeated in every city and its suburbs.

Realising that he was faced with a similar situation which

Armi Sharifuddin had faced in 1948 in the Madiun rebellion, Aidit made his next move – again a copybook manoeuvre. He decided to "go underground" and regroup his tattered organisation, leaving his two principal lieutenants, M. H. Lukman and Njoto to act as the leaders of the "Open Front" of the PKI, hoping that they would hold the President's sympathies for their cause and act as his intermediaries.

Chapter XII

SUBANDRIO BACK IN ACTION

But the Army seems to have got the measure of Aidit. On October 12 Intelligence officers in Djakarta were predicting that Aidit would take six to eight weeks to rally his forces in Central and East Java. They began preparing for the counter-offensive. General Adjie even said that he would "welcome an open offensive by Aidit" so that he could "deal with it in the same fashion as the Madiun communist uprising had been treated". While these preparations were going on the hunt for Aidit was intensified. It seems impossible to the outside world that a man as well known as Aidit could hide successfully from the Army. But Indonesia is an archipelago of some 7,000 islands of which nearly half are scantily populated. Most of this land is still under dense tropical jungle. The Army Command assigned Colonel Sarwo Edhie,* a young tank corps officer with an almost legendary reputation for his success in rounding up political fugitives, to "get Aidit dead or alive", adding with sardonic relish "preferably dead".

On October 6 the *Djalan Rakjat*, a left wing newspaper of Surabaya, published a letter dated October 2 from Aidit to the Greater East Java Regional Committee of the Communist Party:

> "The September 30 event is an internal affair of the Army and the Partai Kommunis Indonesia will not intervene . . . As is well known, it is the consistent stand of the PKI to agree to measures for purification within

*Promoted to Brigadier-General in April 1966 for his services in bringing Sukarno to heel.

all revolutionary instruments and guard the safety of President Sukarno and the Republic of Indonesia. As for the Dewan General, the PKI disapproves of it and condemns it. I call upon all members of the PKI to continue carrying out their tasks, namely to smash the devils."

Colonel Sarwo Edhie traced Aidit's movements from Djakarta to Central Java. On October 2 he had been given a ride in an Air Force plane to Djogjakarta where he had got in touch with Party headquarters. He never slept two nights successively under the same roof. The net was drawing close but for weeks there was no sign of him. By the end of October, Army Intelligence was certain that their quarry was moving towards Solo. But Aidit seemed to be moving very fast. Rumours were about that he had been seen in Surabaya, Madiun, Malan and even as far away as Makassar in the Celebes and Palembang in Sumatra. The most romantic story was that a Chinese submarine had suddenly appeared off a creek not far from Surabaya and had taken Aidit away to a sanctuary in Peking. The Army's purpose was to harry him constantly in order to prevent the PKI from regrouping under his skilled direction.

Colonel Untung was not as lucky as Aidit. He was recognised by two soldiers in mufti who belonged to the Diponegoro Battalion he had once commanded. The *Angatan Bersendjata* told a quaint story of the arrest:

"Untung was unlucky in being captured in a bus named 'Lucky' from Tegal to Semarang in Central Java [*sic*]. When he realised that two of his former soldiers had recognised him he jumped off the bus. But he was caught by the local people who punished him severely for his actions on September 30. The soldiers took him in charge and handed him over to the Army authorities."

The first words he spoke when he was taken to Army

headquarters in Semarang were: "That fellow Bung Karno has let me down." This comment was quickly broadcast and the theory of Sukarno's guilty knowledge of the whole Gerkang received accelerated currency and perhaps played its part in preventing Sukarno from raising a hue and cry about his own conviction that the "Dewan General" had also been trying to oust him.

General Suharto, in pursuance of his orders to "get to the bottom of the coup" took an active part in the interrogation of Untung. It was not a difficult task – judging by accounts of it from Army sources. Untung was tired and bitter about being made a cat's paw by his PKI associates.

While all this was going on, what of Dr Subandrio? It is strange that so many of the major players in the high drama that was climaxed by the Gerkang were away from Djakarta when it took place: Dr Chairul Saleh was in Peking, General Omar Dani probably in Madiun. Dr Subandrio himself was away in Sumatra. When the news of the *coup d'état* reached Sumatra, Subandrio flew back to Djakarta. He explained to reporters that he had returned at once to rally support behind the President and condemn the Gestapu. But the question on everyone's lips was: Why did Subandrio, who was flying in a commercial plane, order the pilot to land at Halim airfield, the Air Force base, and not at the civil airport, Kemajoran, from where he had taken off for Sumatra? Did he fear something? Or did he *know* that Halim was to be the Gestapu's headquarters? Army officers spoke openly about their suspicion – certainty even – that Subandrio had returned to take his prepared place in the Revolutionary Council as the titular Head of State of a PKI administration. Subandrio explained many times to General Suharto that he was innocent of any complicity or even knowledge of the Gestapu but the response was terse: "We have been ordered to get to the bottom of the plot. We are doing so. Your guilt or innocence will be established by the evidence."

It was obvious that the Army was hostile to Subandrio, so he turned on his most subtle performance to wriggle out from under his toppling castles in the air. He took refuge in Merdeka Palace and accompanied the President from Djakarta to Bogor Palace and even from room to room. Suharto was determined to take him away for grilling at Army headquarters, but this was not possible so long as Subandrio was hiding under Sukarno's wing. The Army searched Subandrio's house for incriminating papers but, although army officers who had conducted the raid said that they found enough to convict him, nothing substantial was revealed. General Omar Dani was another refugee in the Palace. Public curiosity, confusion and speculation grew as each day passed.

On October 2 and 3 the Army banned the communist press in Djakarta. The Antara News Agency was closed down until it could be purged of PKI members. The *Harian Rakjat* and the *Warta Bhakti* were given the axe for having hailed the Gestapu as "a patriotic and revolutionary action". The only newspapers now being published were the non-communist Army newspapers, the official organs of the religious parties and the semi-official English language *Indonesian Herald*, well known to be the voice of the Foreign Ministry and Dr Subandrio. The Army newspapers were denouncing Subandrio and Dani for their suspected part in the Gestapu which had been directed, as far as the public had been told, against the President and the Indonesian Revolution. But here were two of the major figures widely accused of complicity, being given shelter and support by the President.

On October 12 the weekend edition of the *Indonesian Herald* published a front page editorial which distinctly showed Dr Subandrio's hand and the direction in which his tactics were moving:

October 1 will be remembered by the people of

Indonesia as a day of national mourning. It was on that morning that the GESTAPU (Gerakan September TigA PUluh) made a violent attempt at changing the structure of the Indonesian Government and to replace Bung Karno as President and Great Leader of the Indonesian Revolution.

Necolim powers rose in jubilation. They had been waiting just for this kind of situation in Indonesia. They had hoped that GESTAPU would unleash in Indonesia a brutal and prolonged civil war between Pantjasilaists and counter-revolutionary elements among the dogmatic leftists in Indonesia. Their spokesman, such as "Minister of Information of Malaysia" had gone on record as predicting that Indonesia would soon see possibility of seeking a settlement with "Malaysia".

But they were rudely disappointed. Thanks to the swift action taken by the Army as headed by Major General Suharto, law and order were immediately restored. Bung Karno was safe and the Dwikora (two-principle) cabinet continued to function as usual. Soon misunderstanding between the Army, the Navy and the Police on the one hand and the Air Force at the other was cleared up. Today, the four armed services are united in one objective: to safeguard the revolution from its enemies, from within as well as from without.

On the political front, Bung Karno, following a plenary cabinet meeting, appealed to the people to preserve calmness while he was personally searching for a political settlement. Bung Karno also appealed to the people to remain on the alert against the number one enemy of the Indonesian revolution: necolim subversion.

Bung Karno's appeal was imbued with a sense of urgency. He had every reason to be concerned about the necolim threat. Because the experience of the Indonesian people in revolution had told them that the danger of necolim threat had been its greatest, as soon as there were signs indicating an impending break in the ranks of national unity. GESTAPU indeed could have brought about that threat, if the Army had not acted promptly.

Let us look at history. The Dutch second military aggression against Indonesia was launched in 1948 immediately after the outbreak of the Madiun affair. Further, when the PRRI rebellion broke out in 1958, contingents of the American Seventh Fleet had made preparations to make a landing in the east coast of Central Sumatra. In this instance, the rapid capture of Pakanbaru by government forces had nipped the sinister plan in the bud.

Today, we are fortunate that the GESTAPU terror movement had been crushed within a matter of twelve hours. The Indonesian people, preserving a cool head, had wisely avoided actions which could have caused a rupture to the national unity. Such a situation would have given our necolim enemies a golden opportunity.

With national disunity avoided, Indonesia can now again concentrate on its most vicious enemy: Necolim forces. "Malaysia", though weakening since the secession of Singapore and severance of diplomatic relations by Pakistan, still constitutes the most dangerous sanctuary of foreign military bases at our doorstep. "Malaysia" and Singapore, though no longer living under one roof, still harbour necolim forces which are hostile to geniune nationalist movements in Southeast Asia.

As such, to Indonesia, confrontation against necolim still constitutes the primary national duty. While we extend our full assistance to the Armed Forces to restore law and order and to punish those responsible for the GESTAPU terror movement, our main energy must continue to be devoted to the execution of DWIKORA. This means the strengthening of the vitality and the extending of aid to the peoples of Malaya, Singapore, and

North Kalimantan to attain true and full national independence from British neo-colonialism.

It is significant to note here that when Coordinating Minister of National Defence and Security and Chief of Staff of the Armed Forces delivered his address on October 4, on the eve of Armed Forces Day, he did not make any reference to GESTAPU. In contrast he dealt at length on the sinister nature of neo-colonialism and the danger emanating from foreign military bases to the freedom of Asia and Africa as well as the imperative need for Indonesia not only to continue confrontation against "Malaysia" but also to extend whatever aid is necessary – including military aid – to nations which seek to secure their national independence.

Indeed, GESTAPU must not be allowed to cause any relaxation in our confrontation against "Malaysia". While the threat caused by GESTAPU to law and order is serious, we must never relax our determination to face the ever increasing danger of necolim subversion interference and intervention."

Dr Subandrio's plan was to detach himself from any formal association with the PKI and the military elements which had participated in or welcomed the *coup*, and to divert people's attention against the stock enemy, the *necolim* scapegoat. As long as he could keep public disquiet directed against a foreign bogey there was a chance to recoup the losses caused by the botched operations of September 30 and October 1. Hence the reference to "The Indonesian people preserving a cool head and wisely avoiding actions which could have caused a rupture of national unity . . . which would have given our *necolim* enemies a golden opportunity." The cool head here referred to the refusal of President Sukarno to ban the PKI despite widespread public clamour for it.

Playing for time in which the seething public agony could

calm down, Subandrio persuaded Sukarno to make a public declaration promising a "political solution" to the problems created by the Gestapu. The idea was that a military solution such as the Army was carrying out against the PKI would end in creating "national disunity" while a "political solution" would resolve the situation so that the old policies of *Nasakom* and *konfrontasi* could be carried on unchanged. Subandrio's brain was as active as ever.

Chapter XIII

MAN-HUNT

General Nasution and his wife were summoned to the Palace during this time to receive the commiseration of the President on their daughter's death. Sukarno's refusal to attend her funeral had caused so much gossip that this gesture was apparently called for. It is also attributed by army sources to Subandrio, whom they contemptuously and openly referred to as a "jackal". Two interesting incidents took place on this occasion.

Sukarno's Japanese wife, Ratna Devi, was present to attend to the obligations of hospitality. Seeing the sadness on Mrs Nasution's face, Devi broke into tears and said: "Bapak, why don't you punish these communists who can do such brutal things to people like this?" Sukarno gently told her "You don't understand these matters. They are more complicated than a woman can understand." Later, Sukarno directly confronted Nasution with complicity in the Dewan General. Nasution grimly denied it. Then Sukarno said "But you were aware of a plan by Yani and his men to take power from me." Nasution denied this too. Sukarno lost his temper and said: "You are lying, you must have known." Nasution then replied: "Bapak, false accusations are even worse than murder." The reference was to Nasution's belief that Sukarno had been responsible for the murder of the generals.

Sukarno's incredulity about Nasution's denial of any knowledge of a plan by the generals to oust him, and Nasution's own resolute refusal to admit to even the possibility of a "preventive action" planned by Yani against the expected death of the President could have a simple explanation: whether it was only a preventive action or more aggressively motivated, General Yani was not likely to have revealed his plans to Nasution with whom he had been on chilly terms since Nasution became Defence Minister.

Nasution and Suharto presented their report on the Gestapu, together with the text of Untung's confession, on October 17. On Nasution's advice, Suharto omitted making any recommendations, leaving it to the President to weigh the evidence and decide on the "political solution" he had promised.

The Army's attitude to the President's left wing protegés was not in doubt. On October 13 General Suharto questioned General Omar Dani in the President's presence about receiving supplies of Chinese arms for the Air Force. When Omar Dani denied this Suharto slapped his face and tore off his epaulettes while Sukarno looked grimly on.

The first part of the "political solution" was given on October 19: the President announced that General Omar Dani was being sent abroad "on an important mission of State". That night Dani left Djakarta secretly for Pnom Penh where he lived until his return in July 1966 to stand trial.

The Army's public image had never been better. It had secured the capital, cleaned out the rebels from Central and East Java and there were daily bulletins about the imminent capture of Aidit. The public was now taking the Army's attack against the PKI into its own hands. The headquarters of the PKI in Djakarta was burned down by a mob of howling students who, in an excess of enthusiasm and compensatory feeling, marched past the U.S. Embassy shouting "Long live America". This was possibly the first time ever that this slogan was heard in South East Asia. Members of the Nahdatul Ulama party of staunch Muslims set fire to the houses of the communist leaders, Aidit,

Lukman and Njono. Lesser communists' property, business houses and trade union offices affiliated to the PKI were similarly destroyed.

At about this time a series of attacks were launched against the Chinese residents in Indonesia who were suspected of having bank-rolled the Gestapu. The "foreign influence" which had provoked the horror of Crocodile Well was now widely regarded as being from "Tjiua". On October 15 *The Times*, London reported:

> ANTI-REDS BURN DOWN A CHINESE VARSITY. Djakarta, Oct. 15: Muslims have burnt down yesterday the Chinese owned Republika University on the outskirts of Djakarta. They had accused the university and its 500 students of being a nest for the movement which attempted a coup against Sukarno's regime a fortnight ago. A Chinese student was reported to have been beaten to death and 250 people were injured in the two-hour riot, during which demonstrators and Chinese students battled with knives, fists and broken furniture. Demonstrators stormed the two-storey building and smashed the contents before setting it on fire. There was shooting for 20 minutes and police arrested about two dozen Chinese students on suspicion of using firearms.
>
> The riot marked the first occasion since the abortive coup that anyone was killed or injured in a series of Djakarta demonstrations.
>
> *The Times*, London.

The *Karya Bhakti* of Djakarta published a charge that Peking Intelligence agents had masterminded the Gestapu and had supplied arms and money to carry it through. An incident in the Hotel Indonesia which purported to substantiate this charge was given nation-wide currency: In the second week of October, a Chinese visitor leapt off the balcony on the 15th floor of the hotel and masses of people watched his remains being scooped off the courtyard below.

Rumour said that he was a Chinese agent who had come from Peking with follow-up instructions and documents which confirmed Peking's criminal intentions toward Indonesia and that he had committed suicide to escape grilling by the Army. The more sophisticated version told by Indonesian newspapermen was that this Chinese was under suspicion and had been followed day and night for many days. Eventually Army agents had begun a deliberate tactic of "leaning on him". They would follow him, close upon his heels, wherever he went, making their presence very obvious. They followed him into the hotel lounge and sat at the adjoining table and waited outside his room door when he went to bed. They were right there in the morning, accompanying him to breakfast. But they never spoke to him. The suspect could not take this any longer and, one afternoon, when his pursuers breath had begun to feel too close and warm on his neck, he fled from them. He took the stairs and they chased after him, up and up and up to the top floor of the hotel. Maddened by days of this kind of persecution, he jumped to his death.

It was a tale that Simenon might have invented. What was singificant here, however, was the explanation behind the deliberate publicity given to it. Among its numerous versions, one stands out for its subtlety: The Army was convinced that Peking was closely involved in the Gestapu but, at that time had very little evidence that would show up incriminatingly in public. They had grilled Lukman and Njoto, the PKI leaders, but they had resolutely refused to talk. Lukman particularly, the tough, hard boiled activist of the PKI, had told his interrogators "Look, I am a communist. Do you think I will ever talk?" Untung's confession contained allegations about Chinese communist connections with the *coup d'état* but nothing that would immediately titillate public interest. The Army plan apparently was to choose a Chinese visitor who was suspected of dealing in black market currency and to goad him to death. It worked out just as they had planned. The story of the Chinese agent was just what the public palate, already jaded by "ordinary" violence, needed. After a few days, its impact diminished and disappeared, but it had served its purpose.

On October 16, 1965, the office of the Chinese Commercial Counsellor in Djakarta was the scene of violent demonstrations by anti-communist mobs. Troops prevented an invasion of the building but some of the soldiers, no doubt excited by rumour and the mood of the mob they were controlling, rapped their rifle butts on the metal work of the locked gates. This action caused Peking to issue the first of its many threatening "Notes" warning Indonesia of "serious consequences" if the agitation against the Chinese residents and Chinese property was not "stopped immediately". Chinese retail merchants in the cities closed their doors for several days until the anti-Chinese fever subsided enough to enable them to make loud protestations of innocence, loyalty to General Suharto and opposition to Peking.

Then occurred the major event in the Army campaign against the communists: Colonel Sarwo Edhie's man hunt for Aidit had begun to seem more like a desparate search for a man-eating tiger. People flocked to this hero of many legends and offered their services as "beaters".

Aidit was moving very fast through Central Java. Road blocks were set up on the main roads and every vehicle was searched. But it is not easy to trap a man in those islands where forests abound and private property is unenclosed. For weeks Sarwo Edhie's Paracommandos followed Aidit's spoor but it was always a day or two late when they found it. Aidit left a trail of rumour behind him but people were apparently frightened to talk about his presence in the area for fear of army action which might damage them or their property. Aidit made an attempt to reorganise his followers from his "Yen An Base" which had been prepared long ago for such contingencies. From nearby Klaten and Bojolali his devotees made contact with him, but Sarwo Edhie was too close for them to do anything but run. With a small band of his followers Aidit made for the Merbabu-Merapi mountains where he apparently expected to lie up and organise resistance. But his pursuers were far too close on his tracks. He then tried to double back to West Java to join up with rebel Brigadier General Supardjo who was continuing resistance with less than a hundred troops. He found it difficult to dodge through the three-ring wall of RPKAD and KOSTRAD troops thrown round Solo. For several weeks it was known that Aidit was in the Solo area.

On November 22* information reached KOSTRAD operations headquarters in Solo that Aidit was holed up in the house of the headman of Sambeng Village, a staunch party supporter. Here again there are many varying versions of what precisely happened. The first part of the story relating to the capture itself does not offer any significant differences. The version that seems most likely to me because it embodies the Indonesian talent for taking serious things lightly, is the story as told by sources close to General Suharto.

Kostrad troops surrounded the house of the headman and a patrol led by a captain made the search. They went right through the house but failed to find their quarry. Disappointed, they were returning through the house when one of them excitedly pointed to something he had spotted. There, on the floor, in front of the doors of a clothing *almirah* stood a neatly arranged pair of wooden clogs. The soldiers smiled as the light dawned on them, then snickered, then bellowed hysterically for several minutes. When they quietened down they whipped the doors open and Aidit stepped out at gun point onto his clogs and was taken away.

At this stage the variations of the story begin to matter more in assessing the part played by Aidit in the Gestapu.

*Indonesian Communists say ruefully that November 22 will be remembered as the day that the "Fortress of Indonesia" fell. "Deepa Nusantara", Aidit's given names, mean just that.

The version current in Djakarta on November 23 was that Aidit was machine-gunned as he stepped out of the cupboard. Another which did the rounds for several weeks was that he was taken to the KOSTRAD camp, put through "a brief interrogation" and executed by a firing squad. The confession published in the *Asahi Evening News* suggests, on the other hand, that the Army took its time before shooting him.

The news of Aidit's execution coursed through the country so rapidly that everyone had heard it by noon next day. The Army command did not try to keep it quiet, nor did they make an official announcement. There was a reason for this. General Suharto was asked by the President to say nothing about it until December 24, the start of the Ramadan festival, when Sukarno promised he would reveal the "political solution" he had promised. Suharto agreed to this apparently on the ground that if the President would make the announcement there would be less chance of an upheaval from the Left. The "simple soldier" of two months ago was already showing signs of becoming a politician. Sukarno's opposition to the Army's demand that the PKI should be banned as a political party was becoming increasingly adamant. Two months after the Gestapu he seemed to become bolder about his protective attitude toward all those suspected of involvement in the *coup*. He tried through speeches and private discussions with Army officials and Indonesian journalists to hammer home the view that he and Subandrio shared: banning and hounding the PKI as the Army insisted on doing was dangerous to national unity; this was what the necolim profoundly hoped for in order to enmesh Indonesia once more in their plots; the Nasakom concept of mutual cooperation in government was irreplaceable.

This intransigence increased his separateness from the Army. Even General Adjie, a devout friend of the President, became estranged. At about this time a quaint document fell into General Suharto's hands: Intelligence officers had found an undated unsigned letter among the papers of the PKI leader Njoto who was also evading arrest when forced to abandon the "open front" tactic. It was a short and cryptic note in the Javanese language: "The goats have been caught and must now be skinned." The Army had no doubt that it was in President Sukarno's handwriting. To Nasution, the explanation seemed simple and positive: for "goats" he read General Yani and the other butchered army generals. Suharto would not accept this interpretation at the start but as Sukarno's attitude to the PKI even after the Gestapu seemed to be inconsistent with the evidence of complicity that the Army had unearthed, he became convinced that Sukarno, together with the PKI, had indeed been in on the plot to kidnap the generals.

Njoto was found in Djakarta and shot dead. The Intelligence officers who arrested him are believed to have invited him to lunch at the Hotel Indonesia – the most expensive meal in the country – and grilled him about the meaning of the "goats" message. When Njoto refused to answer he was taken out and shot. That left only Lukman left out of the PKI troika.*

By early December the campaign against Dr Subandrio, still Foreign Minister, became public. Massive demonstrations were staged, no doubt with Army connivance, demanding the expulsion of the Foreign Minister from the Cabinet, A "White Paper" issued by the government slyly implied that Subandrio was involved in the Gestapu and that he was one of the enemies of the nation. But Sukarno dug his heels in, praising Subandrio in public, and referring to him as the only Minister he had who "could stand up to the necolim".

But the centre of gravity of the concerns of the people in the cities were rapidly shifting from politics to economics.

*Lukman was captured in June at a house in Kebajoran, the near-by satellite town of Djakarta. Rumour says that he too was "liquidated" summarily.

Chapter XIV

STUDENTS AS VIGILANTES

In the wake of the Gestapu came acute shortages of daily necessities. Never before had prices risen so fast or steeply. A litre of rice was now selling at 3500 rupiah but the wage of a day labourer was at 600 to 800. Sugar, tea and chillies had been hidden away by retailers expecting further rises. To help bridge the frightening hole in the budget, the government raised the price of gasoline by 6000 per cent – from 4 rupiah to 250. The allocation of foreign exchange for all the imports needed was drastically cut down to 250 million dollars. That was the maximum available for importing food, raw materials for industry and replacements of machinery. Domestic industry, such as there was, had to cut down production to 20 per cent of capacity. The budget deficit was estimated to be around 1500 billion rupiah. The "open market" rate for the dollar was now between 40 and 50 thousand. Stamp duty, bus and train fares climbed steeply and, by February 1966, were ten times what they were before the Gestapu.

Realising that the economic problems were now getting completely out of hand – even for Indonesia – Chairul Saleh, who was most vulnerable to public criticism because his Ministry was directly responsible for finding a solution, persuaded the President to let him call a "conclave" of some twenty Cabinet Ministers together with the financial-economic experts. Fifty miles away from Djakarta, Saleh had a beautiful hillcountry home at Tjipanas. Here they gathered, guarded by a unit of the Praetorian Guards, the Tchakrabirawa regiment, and for five days they held a non-stop brainstorming session to produce what Saleh called a "Master Plan" to solve the economic problems of the country.

Sukarno, who paid a ceremonial call at Tjipanas, sneered at their efforts and stressed that the real issue was to build up the Djakarta-Pnom Penh-Pyongyang-Peking axis and not to fool around with trivia such as "filling people's bellies". He made a public declaration, with superb disdain, that if any Indonesian dared come forward and offer to solve the economic problems of the country in a year, he would make this brave man a Minister and give him all the authority he needed. If he failed, there would be a firing squad waiting for him.

This kind of bravado might have been effective before the shock of the Gestapu had opened people's eyes to their true situation, but now the University and high school students, like so many of their colleagues elsewhere in Asia, began to take a direct lead in the fight against tyranny, corruption, extravagance and ineptitude. It was the increase in the bus fares that really triggered off this movement to heights of success unsuspected by the students themselves. Chairul Saleh's conclave had formulated the policy of "guaranteeing" forty per cent of the revenues by imposing higher taxes on kerosene and gasoline. When gasoline prices shot up from Rs4 to Rs250, bus fares rose from one rupiah to ten, threatened to rise higher.

In order to minimise the impression of runaway inflation, Chairul Saleh put through the notion of "psychological deflation". The rupiah was accordingly "revalued" by the simple device of dropping three zeros. Thus, a litre of rice which cost 6000 rupiah now seemed to cost only 6. Unfortunately, a wage-earner who was being paid 5000 rupiah now seemed to be getting only 5. This clumsy financial sleight of hand did, however have one salutary result: it reduced the bulk of the package of paper which had to be stuffed into pockets before stepping out of one's home in Indonesia.

Even at this stage of the people's despair, the government was concentrating on appearances rather than on practical ways in which to improve the economic situation. Chairul Saleh told the Press that he was making all arrangements to "provide the extra supply of goods for the coming Lebaran, Christmas and New Year Day festivities". He added: "Stronger discipline is needed to curb the growing amount of money in circulation." What did this mean? Pressed by newsmen (themselves goaded on to active probing by their student friends) to explain what the government really intended to do to improve the material condition of the people following the high power meeting in Tjipanas, Chairul Saleh replied: "A fusing of KOTOE, the Supreme Economics Operations Command and of KOTARI the Command for the Achieving of Self Reliance is now being considered in the framework of the reorganisation of KOTI, the Supreme Operations Command."

The student organisations were no longer agreeable to be fobbed off by this kind of goobledygook. They formed themselves into a militant body they called KAMI* (Kesatuan Aksi Mahasiswa Indonesia) – the Action Front of Indonesia University students. It had an active membership at that time of over 100,000.**

They rampaged in the cities demanding in loud chorus a new deal for the people. Their spectrum of concern stretched from public morality to market prices. Their slogans roundly accused many Cabinet Ministers and public officials of embezzlement and nepotism. They denounced the "Sukarno Establishment" for becoming dollar millionaires (anyone who owned a good fountain pen was already a rupiah millionaire) on bribes and commissions earned abroad and secreted away in banks in Tokyo and Zurich. Some of these Ministers were named and the amounts they

*KAMI also means WE. Another example of the ability of Indonesians to telescope many relevant meanings into a single slogan.

**This figure has now doubled in Djakarta, Bandung, Djogakarta, Surbaya, Bogor and Makassar.

are alleged to have hoarded abroad was anybody's guess, so everybody had a guess. At public meetings Kami orators declared boldly that between four of the most powerful Ministers, 20 million dollars had been stashed away in a Tokyo bank. The students demanded that this money should be brought home to help fill the gaping hole in the economy and quoted the authority of AMPERA – one of Sukarno's own slogans meaning "the mandate that arises from the suffering of the people" – as justification for their demand. The irony of this reference to Sukarno was not lost on their audience. People were already becoming vocal about their disgust over the contradictions between theory and practice in the government.

At about this time Sukarno's Japanese wife, Ratna Devi, was making the headlines in Europe and America where she was blazing an extravagant trail through the fashion houses. In Europe she bought herself a fabulous emerald ring and in New York a blond mink coat. This news was never published in Indonesia but details trickled in and were given swift and widespread currency. Infuriated, the students expressed themselves with a boldness which would have been unthinkable a few months before. On the walls round Bogor Palace they scrawled huge slogans:

WE DON'T NEED JAPANESE DOLLS IN INDONESIA – And then made their point still clearer with another: STOP IMPORTING SECOND WIVES FROM JAPAN.

In front of the Bogor residence of Madame Hartini, Sukarno's third wife, the slogans became coarser: HERE LIVES THE SUPREME PROSTITUTE; THIS IS THE HOUSE OF VD.

During an entire week of January the students ran amok in Djakarta shouting: STUPID MINISTERS GET OUT; ARMY YES – MINISTERS NO.

And now started the kind of direct action which Sukarno and Subandrio had advocated before the Gestapu. They stopped flashy looking Buicks and Mercedes Benzes and daubed paint on them: THIS IS A CAPITALIST.

But their victims were not the "birocrats" that Sukarno had in mind, but his own Cabinet Ministers and close associates who had grown fat under his protection. When the intensity of the demonstrations relaxed, it became clear that KAMI's demands amounted to three:

1. The lowering of prices and taxes.
2. The "retooling" of the cabinet.*
3. The banning of the PKI and its affiliates.

Goaded by the students, the President invited ten leaders of KAMI to attend the Cabinet meeting of January 15 at Bogor Palace in an obvious attempt to put them under his magic spell. It was a disastrous failure. Instead of discussing the demands of the students point by point, Sukarno used the opportunity to insinuate that KAMI was the "tool of the necolim" and that what they were after was not the good of the country but bribes from abroad. He told them that their activities would not cause him to budge one inch. He quoted Martin Luther to indicate his attitude: "Hier Bin Ich; Ich kann nicht anders." He then asked the students to join him as part of the "Barisan Sukarno" – the Sukarno Legions – if they were loyal to him and the Revolution.

When they returned to Djakarta to report to their colleagues, the KAMI leaders were more furious than ever because they had, during that meeting with the President, nearly fallen under his spell once again. Only when they emerged from it had they realised that he had brushed their views aside like troublesome burrs. At the end of the meeting the KAMI delegates had been reduced to asking themselves, as Sukarno wanted, "Are we for Sukarno or against Sukarno?"

The call went out to the country to form the Barison Sukarno – a people's militia which would stand by Sukarno

*Retooling or "ritul" had come to mean change or purge.

against all comers. Subandrio, seeing in this call the chance of remobilising the shattered forces of the Left, offered himself as the rallying point for this movement. There was an immediate and visible response from East and Central Java, but General Ibrahim Adjie, Sukarno's personal friend but political opponent, scotched it firmly with an order from the Western Headquarters of the Siliwangi Division. This order explained that since everyone was solidly behind the President, including the armed forces, there was no point in forming a separate legion of loyalists. Coming from the President's friend, this counter-order was highly effective. Sukarno himself then wriggled out of the confusion he had created by getting Chairul Saleh to explain to General Suharto and to the Press that it had never been his intention to set up the Barisan Sukarno as a separate "physical" entity but only as a "psychological" defence against the threats of the necolim.

On January 18 the President received another visit from the KAMI leaders who, now determined to hold out against his charming wiles, put their three demands to him outright. His answers were brief:

Retool the Cabinet? Who are your candidates?
Ban the PKI? Better wait and see what will happen.
Reduce the prices? What are your suggestions?

The students returned to their headquarters feeling beaten again and convinced that there was no meeting ground between them and the President. They seemed to be talking of different things even when they used the same words.

Chapter XV

STORMKING EXECUTIONS

The mass slaughter of human beings which began soon after the abortive coup increased in intensity as the month of Ramadan approached. At first, it was confined to East and Central Java but, by December, the infection had spread to Bali, Makassar, Sumatra and Sulawesi (the Celebes). In five months between 300,000 and 500,000 people were killed. Initially the deaths occurred as a result of organised clashes between the Army and the supporters of the PKI, including units of the Indonesian armed forces who, ideologically influenced by communism, tried to resist General Suharto's anti-Communist drive by force of arms. There were widespread fears – soon allayed – of a long-drawn-out civil war which would tear the country apart into factions supported from abroad by Peking and Washington. As reports of continued fighting in the hills of Central Java and around Madiun filtered out to the world outside, it seemed for a time as though the PKI might even be able to establish a rival regime in these two regions. It was known that large sections of the KKO – the Marine Corps; the Air Force and the Brimob – the Brigade of Police – had been infiltrated by the PKI and that some of the commanders of these units were, in fact, communists.

The Army acted swiftly to quell the revolt. Strong forces of the Strategic Command and the R.P.K.A.D. paracommandos under Colonel Sarwo Edhie were rushed to East and Central Java in the first few days of October. The Silwangi Division straddled the entrances to Djakarta and kept West Java under control. When Suharto's forces took up their positions, many of the rebel commanders chose not to fight. Only a few like General Supardjo continued their resistance for several weeks. The PKI leaders, knowing that the Gestapu had failed and that President Sukarno had, contrary to their hopes, thrown his weight on the side of Nasution and Suharto, issued orders to their rank and file to lie low. Aidit needed time to regroup his men but, as we have seen, could not stay long enough anywhere to establish a headquarters.

In the first three weeks of October most of the deaths were caused by armed action on both sides. By the end of the month a new army entered the field; the fanatical Muslims who claimed it as their duty to cleanse Muslim Indonesia of atheism. The *santris* in the rural areas – many of them members of the long-suppressed Masjumi Party and the theocratic Darul Islam Movement – who had impatiently watched the communisation process that had been taking place in the past few years, now saw before them the opporunity to establish their own particular brand of obscurantism on the country. They proved to be the most sensitive section of the population to the Army's propaganda drive against the PKI. From the moment the *coup d'état* was foiled, the Army propaganda machine had succeeded in linking it with the PKI. Wall slogans and newspaper headlines constantly referred to that affair as Gerkang/PKI, Gestapu/PKI or Gestok/PKI, driving home the point that the PKI was guilty of the barbarous murder of the generals, the attempt to undermine the Indonesian Revolution and the overthrow of President Sukarno. The fanatics now appeared under the banner of the Nahdatul Ulama, the major legal party of the Muslims. They regarded the lie-low tactics of the PKI as weakness, cowardice and guilt and launched an attack on the communists and their associates which grew through five months into one of the most appalling massacres in human history. The butchery was soon spiritually escalated into a *mujahid* – a Holy War.

The Ulamas – the Religious Teachers – ruled that devout Muslims should regard communists as *kafir habir* – infidels of war – who, according to tradition, had to be put mercilessly to death. They also advised that death by bullet was far too good for the *kafir* and that *kris* and the long-bladed *golok* were more appropriate instruments for the purpose. There was one final ruling: it was *haram* – strictly forbidden – for a Muslim to bury a dead infidel. The crusade against the *kafir* increased in intensity and violence through the months of October, November, December and January.

Tension in Central and East Java had mounted from the third and fourth weeks after the Gestapu, when a rumour was circulated that PKI members were digging large holes and ditches in their back gardens and in the forests to bury their anti-communist neighbours. Army propaganda laid heavy emphasis on the similarity of the Gestapu to the Madiun rebellion, thus pointing up the treachery of the communists. The PKI abandoned its possum posture and retaliated in the first few weeks of November when the death toll mounted rapidly. But their broken ranks could not match the massive fury of the holy warriors and, when the news of Aidit's death reached them, the heart went out of the fight. The angels of wrath were commonly reported to have something more practical than theological righteousness on their side: the paracommandos of the Army who stood by with the same cynicism that the Brigade of Police had displayed during the time when the PKI and its Pemuda Youth Front were fighting their own brand of Holy War. But now it was total war and the cost in terms of human life was immeasurably heavier.

In May 1965, the President, speaking at the celebrations of the 45th anniversary of the founding of the PKI, had hailed the PKI: "Should my kinsman and my brothers die it would be like my own death." It was indeed like his own death. With each unpunished killing that occurred, Sukarno's own authority died a little. As the death toll mounted, he frequently insisted that General Suharto should use the Army to control it. Suharto replied each time that the killings would stop if the PKI was banned so that the people had some assurance of safety from further acts of treachery against the Revolution. When on one occasion, Dr Subandrio supported the President's plea, Suharto stared at him for a long half minute and reminded him that if the Gestapu plotters had won the day, the slaughter would have been much worse and much more brutal in method, following the example given at Halim when the six generals were murdered.

Suharto kept West Java and Djakarta in fair order but could do little to prevent the local clashes in the remoter areas. Rule by decree and infiltration of the law-keeping agencies by political parties had destroyed the tradition of self-regulation that had kept the Indonesian villages in order for centuries. The campaign against the *kafir* soon turned to a free-for-all among local factions which took advantage of the situation to wreak deep-seated vengeance on their enemies. Private grudges were freely discharged.

The killings were given a new name in November when the "holy war" reached its bloody climax: "Stormking* Executions". Suddenly in the night someone in a village would spot the yellow light of a lantern in a paddy field or jungle glade. The entire village would rush toward it to observe the demonic spectacle they expected from previous experience.

The victims would be tied to a tree under the eerie yellow light, and the executioners would stand round them and drive knives into their jugular veins. A witness of some of these events said that the most impressive part of the experience was that many of the victims "went without a whimper" – and he explained with some patriotic pride that this stoicism was possible "not because they were com-

*"Stormking" was the brand name of a hardy paraffin lantern exported by the Dutch.

munists but because they were Javanese. We have learned how to resign ourselves to our destiny." The bodies were left to rot against the trees or were thrown into the nearest open ditch or stream. There are many reliable accounts of rivers in Solo, Sumatra and Madiun being choked with log-jams of human corpses in the months of November and December.

There came a time when the "infidels", at the point of death, began to speak the *Kalimat Sjahadat*, the holy prayer formally acknowledging faith in Allah and Muhammad as His Prophet. Invariably, this testimony would cause the executioners to lower their *goloks* in sudden perplexity. The man was a communist – but now he was also a Muslim and their orders were to destroy the infidel. How could they resolve this dilemma? Evidently, the speaking of the *sjahadat* had been a Party directive since the wave of killings was suddenly halted all along the line in East and Central Java. The crusaders went along to the *Kiaji*, their local teachers of Islam, and sought their ruling. The *kiaji* promised to think about it and let them know their answer within a few days. For a week there was a nationwide reprieve. The wise men thought long and deep about this theological problem and, finally, produced a ruling which ranks besides its Delphic counterparts for its remarkable all-weather flexibility: "Our duty as Muslims is to destroy the *kafir habir*. It is true that they speak the *sjahadat* and thereby, according to the strict letter of the law, are entitled to be regarded as Muslims. But we do not know how sincere they are and we have no means of finding out. Our clear duty therefore is to go ahead and kill them. God knows best. If we have made a mistake, God will forgive them. And us."

The killings were resumed with renewed zeal. On January 15 President Sukarno announced the official tally of the killings following the Gestapu: 87,000. Since official estimates of such events are always much lower than the true figures, the popular reckoning was that 150,000 was nearer the mark. But these assessments excluded the butchery in remoter Bali, Makassar and Sumatra. According to one eyewitness of the course of the anti-communist crusade in Bali, by the end of December nearly 70,000 names had been "erased" from the police register and more than 100,000 known communists had been *diamankan* – "made secure" – and 40,000 more were "scheduled to go". Hundreds of houses belonging to known communists and their relatives and friends were burned down within a week of the crusade being launched in Bali. The occupants were butchered as they ran out of their dwellings. A commonly accepted estimate of the deaths from this operation alone is 50,000 including women and children. All the Chinese retail shops in the towns of Den Pasar and Singaradja were destroyed and their owners were liquidated after summary stand-up judgments were issued convicting them of financing the Gestapu.

In late December General Suharto sent his principal trouble shooter, Sarwo Edhie, to Bali with a strong force of the paracommandos to restore order. Sarwo Edhie told the press that the killings were over by the time he arrived there but there are other reports indicating that the slaughter continued long after. On the basis of Edhie's report to Djakarta, Governor Sutedja of Bali was recalled and accused of preparing a communist insurrection. His relatives were smoked out and killed by the crusaders. The population of several Balinese villages were believed to have been cut in half during the last three months of 1945.

From North Sumatra came a ghoulish report of the slaying of some 10,500 prisoners who had been arrested for PKI activities. Their bodies were thrown into the Sungai Ular. In Medan a public meeting called to denounce the Gestapu was roused to such a frenzy that they marched down to the Pasar, wrecked and burned the Chinese shops and killed 200 Chinese in a single skirmish.

When a rumour was circulated that some students of

religion had been killed by communists, the district of Atjeh experienced a vilent spasm of anti-PKI activity. The number of victims was much more than the estimated number of PKI members in the area. One explanation now offered is that many of the "extra" victims were peasants whose names were on the lists of the Barisan Tani Indonesia, the PKI's peasant organisation. The irony of the story is that many of these peasants had joined the BTI in the belief that they were joining the Barisan Tani Islam – which, according to the Nahdatul Ulama, had been a deliberate trap set by the PKI to snare ignorant villagers.

Mass killing took place in Lombok, Sumbawa, Flores (an island to which Sukarno once, long ago, had been exiled by the Dutch), Makassar, Bandjarmasin and in South Sumatra.

A doctor in Malan, East Java, in charge of relief medical duty, who had also undertaken voluntary duties as protector of the orphans of the district, reported that in his perimeter alone, he and his staff had registered over 400,000 orphans since October.

In January a ministerial commission went around the islands on a fact-finding tour. They publicly announced the official figure of 87,000 dead but their private reports to General Suharto and their friends put the figure as being "probably more than 300,000". In January at the height of the student demonstrations in Djakarta, Dr Subandrio tried to create one of his masterful diversions by trying to get the President to charge General Suharto and General Nasution with the wilful murder of 250,000 to 300,000 people. This attempt was to have serious repercussions for Subandrio two months later when he was arrested and imprisoned by the Army to await his trial on charges of corruption, "selling" Indonesia to Peking and complicity in the murder-plot against the Army Generals.

Most Western diplomats based in Djakarta seem to accept the figure of 300,000 as the probable death tally. This is by no means a safe index to the reliability of these figures.

Many diplomats in such situations become dupes of their own guile. They are prone to pass on their "inside information" to visiting correspondents from their own countries, too many of whom rely on this information because of its "inside" flavour. The information is then passed on to foreign correspondents of other countries who, in turn, pass it on as "inside" stuff to their diplomats who, at the next cocktail party, pass it on to the man who first started the round and, by now, is firmly convinced that his original information was well grounded since it seems to check out from many other sources. This estimate from the Western diplomats of Djakarta is significant only because this is what their own foreign offices have been told and their country's attitudes towards Indonesia are likely to be influenced by this information.

According to Stan Karnow of the *Washington Post*, who shares many of my views about the diplomatic merry-go-round, the number of killings in the five months following October 1, is much higher than that. In April this year Karnow travelled extensively through the areas where the blood flowed freely during the war against the infidels, questioning the local commanders, police, village headmen, hospitals and many other sources. His estimate is that "at least half a million lives were lost".

This holocaust went almost unnoticed by the rest of the world because foreign correspondents were banned or made extremely unwelcome. Many more human beings died in Indonesia in those five months than had died during five years of the war in Vietnam counting the estimated dead on both sides.

It is one of those strange facts of human life that such massive bloodletting, however brutal and painful in human terms, is generally followed by an improvement in the political health of the survivors. The crusade against the infidels of war caused tremendous misery and, in fifteen years' time, someone will have to reckon with the possibly unavoidable desire for revenge among the two million children orphaned under the Stormking lanterns. Politically speaking however, it seems to have served as a catharsis which made it possible for Indonesia to return to the rule of law.

Chapter XVI

A TIME OF MADNESS

Is there a catchall explanation for the mayhem of those five months? People who know and like Indonesia and the Indonesians find it difficult to believe that such brutality, and in such vast proportions, could have occurred in those lovely languid islands. When such things happen there is a common tendency to stick labels on them so that they can be conveniently filed away, out of sight and mind, so that the world may go on to new marvels of human atrocity. C. L. Sulzberger of the *New York Times* was the first to produce the diagnosis which had all the ingredients likely to appeal to the largest common denominator:

"Indonesians are gentle and instinctively polite, but hidden behind their smiles is that strange Malay streak, that inner frenzied bloodlust which has given to other languages one of their few Malay words, 'amok'."

It is temptingly easy to generalise from the particular – by stretching the label which refers to individual aberrations to cover a huge human happening.

The "National Character" label has been used to explain the Stalinist purges, the Nazi atrocities, the Chinese attack on India, the upheavals in the Congo and many other complex human events which, in reality, do not yield to any glib one-piece interpretation. In fact, the significant feature of many of these outbursts of human passion is that they appear to be uncharacteristic. No single observer is likely to produce a complete explanation of the Indonesian purge. It was a climatic event whose causes may be found in many aspects of the social, economic, spiritual, psychological and political life of Indonesia – particularly in the past twenty years.

The intertwining of these various strands of experience produced the events which have been described in the preceding chapters. There are possibly other incidents and circumstances not referred to here which may suggest more profitable directions for inquiry than have been offered. We have seen how tensions in Indonesia were built up to an unprecedented pitch in the days and weeks preceding October 5 – Armed Forces Day. It is clear from the public statements of high ranking politicians and from their private conversations and actions that the Left and Right, represented in the scale of effective power by the Army and the PKI, were sharpening their claws for a bloody conflict. But it was not this which caused the bloodbath that ensued so much as an explosive situation caused by a multitude of events that had taken place over the years on a local and national scale.

Economic privation may explain the tensions in the cities, the public demonstrations and the Gestapu itself; but it does not explain how the killings were centred in the rural areas of East and Central Java, Sumatra and Makassar. The fact that the Army was able to keep a fair measure of control in Djakarta and West Java may indicate that its failure to cope with the problem in other areas – whether it was cynically deliberate or forced upon it – was responsible for the slaughter. On the other hand, it could be argued that if the Army had spread its forces throughout the country there would have been a breakdown of order in the areas nearer the capital, leading to an even bloodier outcome. Also the Army could hardly be expected, as President Sukarno apparently did expect it, to carry out its task of simultaneously fighting and defending the elements which, according to its own convictions, were responsible for the Gestapu.

The Army point of view is that the killings would have

not taken place on such a massive scale if the PKI had been banned as soon as the Gestapu was foiled. This too has only partial validity, since it is probably that Sukarno's sympathy with the PKI acted as a boulder against the wave of anti-communism following the Gestapu. Part of the reason for the mayhem was undoubtedly the widespread revulsion caused by the manner in which the six generals had been butchered and the highly effective use of this news by the propaganda machine. But the primary causes should be looked for in the steady erosion over twenty years of the respect for law and legal process, in the ideological infiltration of the law-keeping agencies, in the ruthless suppression of the political-religious parties, in the tight control of the media of public expression and communication, in the failure of the Sukarno regime to develop the vast potential wealth that lay under its feet, in its preoccupation with Indonesia's world image while domestic problems were swept under a carpet of facile slogans, in the ever-increasing gap between preaching and practice among the people in the upper reaches of power, in the financial corruption at every level of public and private life and last, but certainly not least, in the traditional attitudes and beliefs of the people of Java.

One of the most astonishing experiences of visitors to Djakarta at the height of the mass killings was the apparent indifference among even the most sensitive people to the human tragedy going on in their country. Everyone, including women and children, was excitedly keen on getting the latest news and offering comments and explanations of current events. They would eagerly retail rumours which had come in, hot from the foundry, about decapitated human bodies blocking the streams in Semarang, about human heads ornamenting avenues of wooden spikes along the road to Solo, about entire villages being mown down by a single sweep of the anti-communist militia. But, though there was concern and sympathy for the families of the dead, there seemed to be little horror or sentimentality. It was not the apathetic resignation that one found in Bengal after the Hindu-Muslim riots of 1963, nor the hand-writing revulsion one met in Germany when the atrocities of Belsen, Buchenwald and Dachau came to light, but a kind of positive acceptance of the inevitable.

This sense of the inevitable is a deeply ingrained and familiar trait among the Javanese people. It has its origins and base in the Javanese mystical and spiritual traditions. Most Javanese, from President Sukarno, General Suharto and the Sultan of Djogjakarta down to the village sweeper, believe in and respect the mystical teachings and spiritual methods that abound in the country. One of the customary ingredients of many of them is a profound reliance on prophecy as a guide to human life.

One of the most respected prophets of Java is King Djojobojo (or Jaya Abhaya) who lived in the fourteenth century. He is the Nostrodamus of the Javanese. His predictions are known to every man and woman in Java and their children are weaned on them. According to Djojobojo:

> "After a long period of subjection to a white race, the Javanese will be freed after a yellow race drives away the white race. Then Java will be ruled by a man graced by *sakti* (supernatural power). After twenty years this man will lose his *sakti* and then will come a time of madness in which Java will experience upheavals of such intensity that the population will be reduced to half its previous number, the Chinese will be beaten into a stupor and the white race will be reduced to a pair. After the time of madness, will emerge a new man with *sakti* and a Ratu Adil (prince of justice) whose rule will set the beginnings of a new era of peace, justice and prosperity for the people of Java."

As events unfolded, almost every word of that prophecy, except the references to numbers, has been literally borne out and even those small flaws carried a measure of truth. But what is significant is not so much that the prophecy was proved, but that everyone who knew it believed that it would work out in just that way, and even felt that it was necessary to play his role to fulfil that destiny. The time of madness was therefore inevitable – and indeed necessary – according to this way of feeling and thinking, and the mass killing was not a matter for sentimentality and horror but for sympathetic and courageous acceptance.

Chapter XVII

SUKARNO'S LAST DECREE

On February 21, 1966, President Sukarno announced his long awaited "political solution" to the problems arising from the GESTAPU. It was a brave, but as it turned out, futile attempt to wrest back the power he had lost when he turned over to the Army the job of restoring order after the September 30 affair. In the previous two or three weeks the President and his Foreign Minister seemed to have taken heart and were once more making threatening noises about Malaysia. Dr Subandrio even gave an exclusive interview to Fred Emery of *The Times*, London, in which he hinted at events that would ensue within a few days and would turn the clock back:

> "Djakarta Feb 17: Dr Subandrio, President Sukarno's right-hand man as First Deputy Prime Minister and Foreign Minister, said to-day that he did not think the President 'would succumb to the demands being pressed on him – he does not know if they represent the wishes of the people.'
>
> In an exclusive interview Dr Subandrio told me that the proof that people still had confidence in the leadership of President Sukarno was that he (Dr Subandrio) – and he chuckled over the fact that he had been made the villain by some of the western press – was still there. 'In two or three days,' he said, 'you will see that I am not resigning.'
>
> Evincing further proof of the President's survival, he said, 'If the commanders do not share his views they will

revolt against the President and overthrow him . . . with this anti-communist drive they, the Muslim Parties and reactionaries, have had all their chances – well we survived it.'

Principal points made in the interview were: That the PKI (the Communist Party) would not be banned (believed to be the principal grievance of dissatisfied military commanders, and most political parties).

That China's presence was indispensable for the success of the Conference of the Emerging Forces (CONEFO).

That confrontation against Malaysia 'as the situation now stood' could not be ended by Indonesia, though the 'position is less tense than it existed previously – there is more scope for a political solution'; and a frank recognition that Indonesia's prestige abroad had declined what with 'the *coup*, mass murder, exports at a standstill, and our solvency questioned.'

Cool in his white shirt-sleeved uniform, with four gold stars on his lapel, and as intense and fluent as ever, Dr Subandrio gave all the signs of a confident man."

The political solution was a Presidential Command that the Pre-Gestapu NASAKOM cabinet should be restored – minus Aidit and Njoto who had been killed, and minus General Nasution and Minister-Commander of the Navy, Eddie Martadinata, who had backed Nasution and Suharto. It included Omar Dani who was safely tucked away as a political refugee in Pnom Penh. Subandrio was to retain the Foreign Ministry. Suharto was to continue as Minister-Commander of the Army. Idam Chalid, one of the top leaders of the Nahdatul Ulama, and Hamenku Buwoko, the Sultan of Djogjakarta, were given portfolios to balance the inclusion of the communists. The new Cabinet of ninety-six was once again a coalition of bitter enemies like Suharto and Subandrio at the top, and of time-tested incompetents like Chairul Saleh with the Left's second-string bringing up the rear. Nasution was removed by the elementary device of scrapping KOTI – the supreme executive command of which he was Deputy Chief – and by setting up in its place a new organisation, KOGAM – the Crush Malaysia Command.

The announcement was greeted with a howl of protest from the student organisations, and Djakarta grew tense once more. Wild rumours were on the wing again, with news of rebellion and civil war. These rumours swiftly orbited the earth and in London and Washington, Kuala Lumpur, Delhi and Tokyo that night and on the days following there was hourly expectation that General Nasution would take power forcibly with the support of General Suharto and the Army. But Nasution was not thinking in those terms at all. He no longer had a command. He had no portfolio. He had not even a job or the prospect of one. All he could think about at that time – as he confided later to his friends – was his dead daughter and the sadness of his wife.

Soon after the news was announced, General Suharto and the new Minister for Defence, Major-General Sarbini, called on Nasution and offered to signify their solidarity with him by returning their portfolios. Nasution's answer was characteristic: "No, Bung. You must stay at your posts. I must look after myself. I only want to be left alone for a while."

Suharto ordered that Nasution should continue to be paid his general's salary and should retain his office and other privileges. He consulted the Sultan of Djogjakarta and other close friends and decided to protest against the inclusion of the communists in the new Cabinet, but the President was adamant. The one thing that seemed to sustain Suharto was the advice of his *guru* who had told him that despite all Sukarno's efforts to thwart destiny, power must desert him and reside with Suharto and the Sultan of Djogjakarta who was already widely identified as the Ratu Adil, the prince of justice of the Djojobojo prophecy. Suharto even believed that Sukarno's decision to bring the Sultan into the cabinet was proof of the fact that despite himself the President was playing his part in the ineluctible development of destiny by bringing his successor near to the centre of power.

The *guru* had explained that beneath and beyond the coarse human feeling that everyone has, there is a finer and more sensitive feeling known as *rasa*. The spiritual purpose of man is to find, develop and know this *rasa*. The bond between Suharto and his *guru* was established through this *rasa* being transmitted by the *guru* to the pupil. According to the indications given by this inner feeling Suharto, in the immediate future, had to play his *lakon*, or ascribed part, in directing the destinies of his country in close alliance with the Ratu Adil. Suharto had to play the role of a general in paving the way for the rule-fulfilment by the Sultan of Djogjakarta. And the two men, being *sarasa* – that is, sharing the same *rasa* or being harmonious in their inner feeling – would be able to outmanoeuvre Sukarno, Subandrio and any others who blocked their path.

The instruments of destiny were to be the students of Djakarta. Their demonstrations protesting against the dropping of Nasution and Martadinata and the inclusion of Subandrio, Saleh and Dani in the new Cabinet, became increasingly shrill as the days dragged on and February limped into March. Their demands were, as before: retool the cabinet, ban the PKI and all its affiliates and reduce prices. But their campaign became much more personal and pointed in detail. Their placards and wall slogans abused Subandrio and Dani and demanded the return of the non-communist Ministers to the Cabinet. This meant the punishment of corrupt Ministers, and elimination of Subandrio and Chairul Saleh. They accused Subandrio of being a paid agent of Peking. As the days wore on they swarmed all over Djakarta, concentrating their numbers and their most telling slogans round Merdeka Palace.

Every available inch of wall and road space was scrawled with anti-Subandrio slogans. Never before have I experienced such a concentration of hatred against one human being.

HANG SUBANDRIO – FRY SUBANDRIO – KILL SUBANDRIO – BANDRIO BANDIT – "RETOOL" SUBANDRIO – GANTUNG BANDRIO – GANTUNG BANDRIO – GANTUNG BANDRIO. And the most vicious of them all: BANDRIO ANJING PEKING – which meant: Subandrio is a Peking dog, a pekinese. Subandrio took shelter once more in the Palace in fear of his life and stuck close to the President night and day.

The first meeting of the new cabinet was a major fiasco. The students blocked the street and the palace gates. The new Ministers had to be air-lifted in by the President's helicopter. Only half the number dared attend even then.

President Sukarno called a press conference on February 21 to explain his action. He was anxious to convey the impression that the new Cabinet was a necessary and integral part of the Indonesian Revolution: "I had contemplated this reshuffle a long time ago but it could not be carried out because of political unrest. Its tranquility has never been restored, the reshuffle has now been made." Then almost in an aside he revealed the real motivation behind his move: "The functions of the new Cabinet will be different from the old liberal practices. New Cabinet Ministers are to *assist* the work of the President who is Mandatory of the MPRS (People's Consultative Congress)."

More concentration of power at the centre. "Liberals" like Nasution, Martadinata and Ibile Gandamana who had served as Minister for Rural Development were excluded because they were bound to be difficult for Dr Subandrio to handle. This was the central point. The enhanced powers of the President would not be used by him in the day to day decision making and executing of policy but by his Grand Vizier, Subandrio.

Sukarno's henchmen – Subandrio and men like General

Achmadi, Minister of Information – turned on propaganda calculated to show that Nasution and the "liberals" had been pawns of the *necolim.* Achmadi told the correspondent of the Yugoslav newspaper *Borba*:

"The political solution of the counter-revolutionary *Gerkang* is not merely the dissolution of the PKI. At present it is to safeguard the Indonesian Revolution from the assaults of the *necolim* and their attempts to shift its course to the right."

As soon as the new Cabinet was announced Subandrio gave a clear indication that he would swiftly undo some of the major decisions that the Army had taken in bringing about relative tranquillity. He would use his powers to "settle the cases of the civilian prisoners connected with the *Gerkang*" he said, adding: "The settlement will be just – in accordance with the instructions of the President."

An all-out effort was now made to wash away the mud flung at the President's public image by the KAMI students. Subandrio and Brigadier General Amir Machmud, Commander of the Djakarta Garrison – another Sukarno loyalist – organised what they called a "Guard Roll Call" at Lapaugan Banteng. Antara reported that over one million people attended the meeting at which Machund declared the people will "rise or fall with Bung Karno". Subandrio's speech was directed toward giving the crowd a local target. By evident prearrangement, a mob of youths of the Pemuda Front once again performed their act outside the American embassy at Merdeka Selatan. They climbed over the iron fence and entered the premises carrying placards and shouting slogans at the new American Ambassador. "Go to hell Green", "Green masterminded to topple Bung Karno", "Green CIA Agent", "Hidup Bung Karno."

Subandrio's editorial writers shifted their sights again. The *Indonesian Herald* chuckled:

> This new step taken by Bung Karno – one in a series

which can be classified into the overall political solution – has dealt a stunning blow to the wishful thinking in Kuala Lumpur and London which had been dreaming of a "withering away" of Indonesia's confrontation against *necolim* domination in South East Asia as personified by 'Malaysia'.

Monumental efforts were made in the Prime Minister's Office – which Subandrio, as First Deputy Prime Minister administered – to reform the tattered regiments of the left-wing student organisations. Army sources believed that Subandrio was authorised to spend up to 300,000,000 new rupiah, which were hurriedly printed on a special order of the President, to finance a student force to counter the KAMI. There were several scuffles and skirmishes between KAMI groups and the pro-Subandrio student groups. KAMI leaders complained that the opposition was being armed by Subandrio but this only served to infuriate the KAMI rank and file. The slogan war against Subandrio and the new Cabinet was intensified.

On February 26, the President, goaded by the mockery of the students, banned KAMI (The Action front of the University Students of Indonesia). The order read:

> The President-Supreme Commander of the Armed Forces Supreme Commander of the KOGAM in his decisions on the dissolution of KAMI stated the following:
>
> The disbanding of KAMI is effective as of February 26, 1966.
>
> Student demonstrations of any kind, including a gathering of more than five persons, are prohibited.
>
> Severe actions will be taken against violation of the point on the ban on student demonstrations – gathering of more than five people.
>
> Similar stern actions will be taken against anyone – any group extending assistance – giving opportunity to students to stage any demonstration.

All Pepelrada's (Dwikora administrators) in the country are called upon to execute this decision.
This decision takes force as of the date of its issuance, namely on February 26, 1966.

But KAMI students would not stay banned. Overnight their numbers in Djakarta were re-inforced by their colleagues from the other University towns. They were given additional moral force by the formation of KASI – the Action Front of Intellectuals established by their professors and lecturers.

Apparently to boost the morale of the President and repay him for giving a Cabinet post to Dr Idam Chalid, one of his loyalists in the Mahdatul Ulama party, a new title was confirmed on him: Pembingbing Agung Alun Ulama Seluruh Indonesia (Supreme Leader of the All-Indonesia Islamic Clergy). The propaganda sheets declared over and over again that "Bung Karno's position had never been so strong."

Djojobojo and Destiny were not, however, to be baulked so easily. The banning of KAMI proved to be the biggest tactical error Sukarno ever made. It was this decision that unleashed the most formidable enemy that he had ever faced in his fifty years experience as a revolutionary: the children of Djakarta, unarmed and unafraid, formed themselves into a new movement called KAPPI and stepped into the streets to carry on the struggle begun by their elder brothers and sisters. The youngest among them were eight and nine, the oldest fifteen, but they seemed to have a political consciousness one would expect of men and women of thirty.

Chapter XVIII

THE CHILDREN'S REVOLUTION

It was the cynicism of Sukarno more than anything else which annoyed the young students. The blatancy with which he had packed the new Cabinet with GESTAPU associates first caused incredulous astonishment, then fury. Student leaders declared that the President had shown supreme contempt for public opinion by going directly against the grain of mass feeling. Perhaps the most remarkable instance of Sukarno's cynicism was the appointment of Imam Sjafii as Minister for Security of the President. Not only was he closely associated with the GESTAPU, but he was also nationally known as the leader of the Cobra Gang – the most vicious and active underworld characters – specialising in murder, armed robbery and blackmail. Another appointment which caused widespread annoyance was that of Asmara Hadi, as Minister-Vice-Chairman of Parliament. Hadi's sole qualification for the job was that he had married Sukarno's adopted daughter. Nepotism at a time like this was regarded by the students as an unpardonable offence.

Tempers rose so high that a group of students who had attended the "Grand Roll Call" meeting at Lapangan Banteng at which the President's policies were expounded and explained by Subandrio and Achmadi, marched directly to the Palace to display their anger. Djakarta that afternoon was again tense and taut. There had been a *lindu* – an earth tremor – the day before and Indonesians regard this as an ominous sign. Events seemed to vindicate this belief. As the students approached the Palace, the Tchakrabirawa guards blocked their way. A scuffle ensued and, n thei general frenzy, one of the guards let loose a burst of fire – killing one student and wounding eight others. The skirmish ended. There was a moment's pause as both sides realised what had happened. The guard who had fired the shots panicked and rushed towards the Palace gates for protection. Before he reached sanctuary, he was killed by a bullet from a soldier in the Army unit standing by.

The students took the body of their dead colleague, Arif Rachman Hakim, for burial. A million people, parents and students, attended the funeral. Hakim was proclaimed as *Pahlawan Ampera* – Hero of the People's Suffering. Mrs Yani, the widow of General Yani, delivered the funeral oration, adding to the sense of desperate times by her presence.

The younger boys and girls who had organised themselves into KAPPI – (Kersatuan Aksi Permuda Perlaja Indonesia) – the action front of the high school students, were even less inhibited than their elder brothers and sisters in KAMI, the University students action front). Their first target was the new Minister for Basic Education, Dr Sumardjo, reputed to have played an intimate role in the GESTAPU. New slogans sprouted overnight: RETOOL THE ATHEIST – EXPEL THE GESTAPU FROM THE CABINET.

At this stage, Sukarno and Subandrio encouraged the students organisation of the Partai Nationalis Indonesia, the ASU, to make a fight for the leadership of the student movement. Subandrio told a meeting of ASU youth that "Terror must be met by terror" and Sukarno said "The dogs may bark but the caravan moves on". Immediately the KAPPI sloganeers produced a new country-cry: ASU-DOGS. Asu is a Javanese word for a cur.

On March 3 KAPPI demonstrators occupied the auditorium of the Education Department at Djalan Merdeka Timur, declaring it to be their headquarters from then on. Their teachers announced on March 5 that they had formed themselves into two organisations to carry on the struggle started by the students: KASI (Kersatuan Aksi Sardjana

Indonesia) – the action front of the scholars, and KAGI (Kersatuan Aksi Guru Indonesia), the action front of the teachers.

On March 8 KAPPI demonstrators waged their first major battle. Their target for the day was Dr Subandrio and his Foreign Ministry. They were looking for documentary evidence of his involvement with Peking. They marched in, singing songs and shouting slogans. The Djakarta garrison under General Machmud, who had become one of the embodiments of repression and cruelty as far as the students were concerned, threw tear gas at them. There was pandemonium. The students ran amok through the building breaking windows and furniture, ripping the drapes (to wipe away their tears, they said afterwards), tearing file-covers and every piece of paper they found. They broke open locked cupboards and desks and chucked their contents out on the street. The guards dared not open fire; the memory of the reaction to the shooting near the Palace was too fresh for them to risk another incident. Within an hour, the Foreign Ministry was a shambles. Nothing had been left intact.

Walking past the building that evening I wondered how Subandrio's bureaucrats could ever work again. What do bureaucrats do without papers and precedents? Where would they start? Would they buy a new file-cover, label it "Crush Malaysia, March 9th, 1966" and send it up to Subandrio for a brand new minute? Imagine Whitehall, Pennsylvania Avenue, the Quai D'Orsay or Raisina Hill in New Delhi littered with confetti made from documents marked CONFIDENTIAL, SECRET, MOST SECRET, FOR YOUR EYES ONLY, dating from the year zero.

The students claimed that they had found the papers they were looking for – documentary proof that Peking had masterminded the GESTAPU. But this turned out to be nothing more serious than a boost for their own morale. It was not likely that Dr Subandrio would have left any incriminating papers of that nature in the relatively unprotected Foreign Ministry when he spent most of his time in the well-guarded offices allotted to the Prime Minister. But the students paraded the streets claiming they had discovered evidence of the "Secret Canton Pact" by which Subandrio was widely alleged to have "sold Indonesia to Peking". People believed the story because, at that time, they liked to believe anything that damned Subandrio.

On the next morning Sukarno, accompanied by Subandrio and Chairul Saleh, inspected the damage at the Foreign Ministry and remarked in an aside intended for the ears of the reporters who were following them at a discreet distance: "If this is not counter-revolutionary action dictated by the *necolim*, what is it then?"

The Indonesian *Herald* reported:

"Djakarta, March 10 (*Herald*): Tuesday's riot by students and secondary school pupils inside and outside the Foreign Office building at Pedjambon effected heavy security and material losses, officials of the Department of Foreign Affairs told newsmen yesterday.

"President Sukarno in spite of his busy schedule showed his personal interest by visiting the Foreign Office Wednesday to inspect the damages caused by the rioters.

"After having seen the damages done to the building and offices of the Department of Foreign Affairs, President Sukarno stated to newsmen who were covering the occasion that it was no more the work of innocent school children, but through the use of innocent children somebody or somebodies have conducted the act of subversion [*sic*].

"This is no more a political game, but downright counter-revolutionary," he said.

When this statement was conveyed to KAPPI, the students became enraged at the continuing suggestion that they were the pawns of some foreign power when, in their opinion, it was men like Subandrio who were obviously acting as foreign agents.

On March 10 their attacks were directed at Communist China's offices in Djakarta. They demonstrated outside the Chinese Consulate at Kramat Raya and the House of Culture of the People's Republic of China in Djalan Tjilosari. They set fire to the offices of Hsin Hua, the New China News Agency in Djalan Tanah Abang Bukit. In eight months the wheel had come full circle.

That night the President summoned the leaders of the political parties and demanded that they should jointly condemn the student demonstrations in a signed statement. The religious parties complied. When the statement was released that night there was so much resentment among the students and their parents that Nahdatul Ulama messengers had to spend the rest of the night explaining to the student leaders that they had been forced to sign.

General Suharto, however, refused to agree to the President's request that he should condemn the student activities on the radio and television services. Suharto was well aware of the dangers of anarchy. But as the demonstrations continued and it was clear that the parents of the students and their teachers supported them, he began to feel that this was a genuine people's movement. Suharto and the Headquarters Command had been busy during the past two or three nights preparing an operational plan. The Java commanders met and agreed to Suharto's proposal that the Army should support the students. The only murmur came from General Ibrahim Adjie, the Commander of the Siliwangi Division in West Java, who told Suharto: "I am as stoutly opposed to Sukarnoism as you are. But if one hair of his head is touched, you will have to fight the Siliwangi." This held Suharto and the younger activists like Sarwo Edhie back from making an immediate putsch. Adjie was a loyal friend and a formidable opponent. They respected his loyalty to the Bung but resented his obduracy about taking any action against Sukarnoism that might in any way hurt Sukarno. The night of March 10 must have been for Suharto what the night before the execution of Charles I must have been for Cromwell.

Suharto, whose character as we have seen is deeply ingrained with *kebatinan kedjiwan* – Javanese spiritualism – was confronted by the grand dilemma that all sensitive regicides have experienced. Brought up to believe in the traditions of the *Satrias*, the traditional knights of Java, he accepted the chivalric code, and one of the tenets of this code was:

Tinigas sumangga djangga
Kabanda sumangga asta
Setya-tuhu marang guru lan ratu

It means:

May my throat be cut
May my hands be tied
I remain loyal to my guru and my king.

Suharto felt that his loyalty to his *guru* was more profound than his duty to his "king". As a soldier and a Javanese he valued the contribution Sukarno had made to the liberation of Indonesia and, as a practical man, he realised the dangers involved in alienating Ibrahim Adjie, in risking an open conflict with Sukarno who, he was sure, would have the support of the leftwing millions who were now waiting underground for their day to dawn again, and from substantial elements of the Police, Marine Corps and the Air Force. But his *guru*, to whom he felt he owed his successes up to date and even his survival, had advised that it was now time to act and fulfil his destined role of bringing about the changes his country needed. The spiritual conflict could only be resolved if the *ratu* was identified as someone other than Sukarno. And, since he was aware that the Sultan of Djogjakarta had the necessary spiritual and temperal lineaments, and that they shared a common fate, the dilemma was resolved. Suharto decided to go ahead and take the military risks that his decision entailed.

By March 11 the students had brought Djakarta to a standstill. Every morning tens of thousands of boys and girls would gather in the centre of the city, along the grand road leading to the Asian Games Komplex and at the main entrances to Djakarta. When the traffic began to move, they stood across the street, forcing the first hundred vehicles to a halt in four or five lanes. When a fair number had been halted, platoons of children scampered through the melée, deflating the tyres. By this time hundreds of vehicles would be piling up in the rear and the children would drift away laughing, to reform ranks and march along to the Palace. Some of them piled into trucks and jeeps which they had commandeered to convey them within the city, shouting slogans, singing lampoons composed on the wing, denouncing Subandrio and the new Cabinet. A visitor from Mars would have imagined that it was a national holiday. Even the monstrous tanks prowling about the streets served as props in the picnic scene. The children clambered aboard, offering to share their food and drink with the soldiers, and riding the guns. They darted up and down with the impudence of water birds pecking about in the mouth of a crocodile.

The special court set up by General Suharto to try Colonel Untung and Njono had just announced its verdict: the death penalty for both. They had both pleaded that they had been acting against the "Council of Generals" but the court found no evidence of such an organisation except the "normal committee which dealt with such matters as promotions of officers". President Sukarno was reported to have interceded with the tribunal in an attempt to secure a softer verdict but he had failed. He then ordered a stay of the execution until he gave his order. This development added fuel to the fire now raging in Djakarta.

On the morning of March 11 President Sukarno called another meeting of the Cabinet. Only half the number of Ministers were able to attend: thirty-one of them had slept the night in Merdeka Palace and others had been flown in by helicopter while the students below jeered and waved their fists at the aircraft. Sukarno opened the meeting with his customary monologue. They had all heard it before but the situation outside seemed to give special weight to the President's briefing. He spoke about the need to intensify the Revolution, the need to prevent the Indonesian Revolution from swinging to the Right, the need to carry on the struggle against the *necolim*; and he then proceeded to outline the task of each Minister. Clad in T-shirt and slacks, with his shoes shucked off under the table, his feet resting in a pair of bedroom slippers, Sukarno seemed to be relaxed and self-assured. Not so Subandrio and Chairul Saleh who flanked him. Subandrio had also taken off his shoes but people observed that his toes were twitching nervously. The reason for his agitation may have been the absence of General Suharto and the Sultan of Djogjakarta.

A few minutes before noon Police Commissioner Sumirat, one of the Presidential aides, approached Sukarno and handed him a piece of paper. The President read the note and immediately called for his jacket. He whispered something to Dr Leimena, the Second Deputy Prime Minister, and hurriedly left the chamber without a word of explanation. He was so excited that he did not wait to put on his shoes. Carrying his slippers in his hand, Sukarno rushed out toward the helicopter waiting on the lawn. Subandrio spoke to Commissioner Sumirat, then to Chairul Saleh, and the two Ministers hurried after the President. Subandrio was in his socks as he ran out leaving his shoes under the table. An observer of these events later remarked that "This was a clear example of the meaning of the Dutch saying: *een held op sokken*" – a 'hero in his socks' or a coward.

A moment or two later the Ministers heard the sound of

a helicopter taking off. Johannes Leimena took the chair and tried to go on with the meeting but no one paid much attention. They were all wondering about the source and contents of the note which had caused the three top men in the government to fly away so precipitately. That note will be one of the historical documents of Indonesia. It was even briefer than the four line proclamation of Independence which Sukarno had written on a scrap of paper in 1945.

It read: *The Palace is now surrounded by irregular troops.*

The question of the authorship of the note has not yet been settled. Two opinions predominate: that it was written by Brigadier General Mohammad Sabur, the new commander of the Tchakrabirawa Regiment guarding the Palace, or that it was sent by General Suharto. Sources close to Suharto prefer the first, pointing out that Suharto that afternoon was in bed suffering from a severe cold and an attack of ancina. But the "operational plan" he had devised had been carried out in the past two days. On the pretext of guarding the President against the onslaught of the students, General Suharto had thrown three rings of his own men round the Palace. On the morning of March 11 two curious phenomena caught my attention. The third ring encircling the Palace was composed of strategically placed mortars – all pointing *towards* the Palace – and there were hundreds of Sarwo Edhie's paracommandos manning the second ring, many of whom had stripped off the "distinctives" from their uniforms.

That afternoon there was furious military activity in Djakarta and Bogor. The paracommandos used their tanks to surround the barracks of the Tchakrabirawa Regiment, located close to the Palace. KOSTRAD and RPKAD forces staged a massive "show of force" in the two cities. The show was ostensibly directed against the demonstrators but no one doubted that the message was intended for the President.

This was the significance of the note the President had

received. The helicopter took the President towards Bogor but touched down in the village of Tjilandak, about fifteen kilometers from the city, where the President alerted a unit of the KKO – the pro-Sukarno Marine Corps stationed there – to watch for an Army *coup d'état.* At Bogor the show of force by Sarwo Edhie's troops was in full swing when Sukarno reached his palace. There he retired to his study and sulked while Madame Hartini entertained his two guests.

* * *

A flashback is necessary to explain the events that occurred that day outside the Palace. Here is the account of the activities of one of the principal players as given to me by an Indonesian journalist with access to the inner councils of the Army, the Nahdatul Ulama and the other political parties. General Amir Machmud, head of the Djakarta Command, had played a curious role in developments since the GESTAPU. He was friendly with General Suharto, General Nasution and others who were opposed to the pro-Peking policies of Sukarno and Subandrio. Machmud had never been associated too closely with the PKI but he had leaned heavily to the side of the President and Subandrio in their efforts to prevent a swing to the Right. In fact, he had provided the military cover for the Grand Roll Call and had done everything in his power to suppress the student demonstrations. His public stance was that, as a soldier, he was carrying out the orders of the President, his Commander-in-Chief. At the same time he was doing his best to keep in well with the Army and the Nahdatul Ulama, the two strongest organised forces in the country. He had coined the term "Flat Tyre Democracy" to label the students' activities as irresponsible and anarchistic. But, in his dealings with General Suharto, he gave the impression that he sympathised with the demands of the students – that

Subandrio should be driven out of the Cabinet and that the Cabinet should be purged of the vestigial remains of the *Gerkang* of September 30.

General Machmud was in the Palace when the Cabinet session was on. Later he gave the leaders of the Nahdatul Ulama the following story:

> When the President rushed out toward the lawn, I escorted him to the helicopter. I said to the President: "Bapak, I am grieved about all this."
>
> The President seemed, for the first time, helpless. He held my hands firmly and stammered: "*Kemana aku, Amir? Kemanu aku?*" (Where shall I go Amir, where shall I go?) I was deeply moved to see the President in such a state. The President departed for Bogor, leaving me in tears.

Military commanders from various parts of the country had arrived that day in Djakarta to be present at the *musjawarrah* and briefing that had been scheduled to take place at the Palace on March 12. They were all assembled that afternoon at Army headquarters. Machmud himself was present. General Suharto, still encumbered by his cold, conducted the meeting. The Young Turks like Sarwo Edhie and Remal Idris were for taking a strong line against the President. Some suggested the "elimination" of Sukarno, Subandrio, Chairul Saleh and Sumardjo.* They wanted "a clean break with the past". One commander suggested "doing a Farouk on the Bung" – sending him into exile with sufficient money to enable him to spend the rest of his life with any or all of his wives, on the Riviera or wherever he chose. Ibrahim Adjie was becoming more and more obviously miserable as the discussions became strident. The concensus of the meeting was that it was time to call a halt to the efforts of the President and Subandrio to resusi-

*One member of the triumvirate is credited with the remark: "Let's give them a fair trial and shoot them."

tate the discredited Peking-oriented policies and to bring Indonesia and its capital to order.

Finally it was Suharto's presence and eloquent reticence that predominated. His proposal that emissaries should be sent to Bogor to negotiate a new deal with the President was accepted. With considerable acuity, he nominated three senior commanders to undertake the assignment: General Amir Machmud, General Basuki Rachmat, formerly the commander of East Java, the General Andi Mohammad Jusuf, now Minister of Basic Industries, formerly commander of South Celebes, who was reputed to have been responsible for the elimination of the rebel Darul Islam gangs.

There was admirable subtlety in the choice. The three men were regarded as being "softer" on Sukarno than anyone else present. They would be the most likely to be trusted by Sukarno – Machmud because he had taken stern action against the students and the others because of their background as tough and able soldiers who had never been identified as being overtly leftist or rightist. A document was prepared in outline which would effectively give General Suharto, as Minister Commander of the Army, the executive authority he needed to "bring Djakarta and the whole country to order". The three men were asked to present it to the President and "ask him for his blessings".

Late that night Amir Machmud gave Idan Chalid and other leaders of the Nahdatul Ulama a blow-by-blow account of what took place:

> "General Suharto assigned us to go to Bogor to 'put the President's mind at rest'. The General said: 'tell the President that he need not worry about anything, whatever happens.' As we motored to Bogor we spoke very little. We were wondering what to say and how to say it to the President. Silently we were praying, asking God to give us His guidance, strength and the right spirit to

meet the President. When we sat in the presence of the President we did not broach the subject of our visit at first. We indulged in small talk. The conversation just wandered on. Then, at one point, without fully realising the full implications of it, I said casually to the President: 'Bapak, the times are very difficult and you are so much overburdened already. Why not let us handle the job?' To this the President replied 'Will you be able to do it?' I answerd, simply, 'yes'. The President replied: 'All right then, draft out an Order.' At this stage Madam Hartini intervened and said: 'Indeed, Bapak is very tired nowadays. Why not let them do the job?' The President retired to his room and the three of us then prepared the Order according to the outline we had received. We took it to the President who read it, nodded approval and then signed it saying '*Bismillah*' (In the name of God). We did not expect things to turn out this way at all. It was quite astonishing."

The Nahadaul Ulama were deeply touched by this story and remarked saidly: "*Kasihan Bapak*" (poor Father). But, moving as it was, Amir Machmud's story was a dressed up version of the truth, designed to curry favour with the Ulamas. If the President's capitulation could be seen as submission to God's will rather than to pressure brought to bear by mere mortals the Ulama could accept what had taken place as divine intervention in the affairs of Indonesia. Machmud knew that they were uneasy because, having earned a Cabinet post from the President, they were now faced with the chance of losing their status under a Military government. He exercised true diplomacy.

In point of fact, the three generals had carried with them an ultimatum from General Suharto. If the President had rejected it, there would be a powerful "show of force" by the Army on the following day, and he would have been compelled to capitulate and risk exile or execution. The most effective threat, however, was that he would be humiliated publicly if he did not acquiesce. For a man with such an ego as Sukarno's this must have seemed a fate far, far worse than death.

What in fact happened was that when the generals suggested that times were bad, Sukarno asked ruefully what could be done. Andi Jusuf's response was: "only Suharto can control the situation." The President asked: "How can he do it?" Jusuf replied: "He can if you give him authority to act in your name." The order which had been drafted by the Army command was then produced and Sukarno realised that the game was up. As he was about to sign, Subandrio asked to see the document, read it and commented: "But this means handing over all powers to Suharto!" The President said tersely: "Agreed," and put his name to the executive order empowering General Suharto to act in the name of the President in order to bring about law and order in Indonesia.

At midnight General Suharto announced over Radio Indonesia that he had been given executive authority by the President to take all measures needed to maintain public security and calm. His first executive act was to ban the Communist Party and all its affiliates. Sukarno had resisted this move to the end. He had no wish to go down into history as the man who banned the PKI, nor did he relish the reactions against this move from Peking and the socialist countries. But the ban was effected under his hand by his "Mandatory", General Suharto.

The Orders of the Day also denounced the GESTAPU and its remnants still active in public life; rejected the decision of Sukarno's Minister of Education to close down the Djakarta University whence KAMI had sprung; paid a tribute to the *Pahlawan Ampera*, Arif Rachman Hakim, the student who had been killed by the Tchakrabirawa; and confirmed the death sentences passed on Untung and Njono.

On March 12 Djakarta was in carnival mood. The show of force which the Army had planned to take place that day was transformed into a triumphal march. KOSTRAD and RPKAD tanks roared victoriously through the city while a million boys and girls marched the streets shouting victory slogans and singing Indonesian pop songs. The soldiers shouted: "HIDUP KAMI, HIDUP KAPPI" and the children shouted back "HIDUP ABRI (long live the Armed Forces), HIDUP PAK 'HARTO (Father Suharto)." Bunches of flowers and red-green *rambutans* were tossed into tanks and armoured cars. Children rode into town from the outlying suburbs and villages, a dozen of them clinging precariously on to each passing vehicle. "Uncle, will you take us into town?" was the disarming request. There was no denying it. One group of boys hopped off the top of a truck when they saw a covey of nuns of Dutch origin, now Indonesian citizens. They surrounded the nuns and shouted: "HIDUP JESUS CHRIST." And so it went on till late at night and started all over again next morning.

Here and there, there were discordant shouts: GANTUNG BANDRIO (Hang Subandrio) . . . GANTUNG DURNO. The older student leaders were conscious that only one of their demands – the banning of the PKI – had been achieved. The retooling of the Cabinet and the expulsion of Subandrio, Chairul Saleh, Sumardjo and others connected with the Gestapu were still to come. They therefore interlarded their victory slogans with demands for the completion of their programme.

Chapter XIX

THE TRIUMVIRATE BEGINS

For General Suharto the way was not easy. He was now in effective control but the threat of a massive reaction from the suppressed leftwing was always present. And running a government – even a bad one – is a much more difficult operation than taking power. The Army had no experience in handling foreign affairs, economics and finance. Who could he get to undertake these hideously complicated tasks for him? General Nasution was the ablest of his more prominent associates, but he was still brooding. He had been kept fully informed of what was going on but had not come out to join the fray. The Sultan of Djogjakarta was a great source of strength. His reputation as socialist prince, a competent administrator and a man of profound integrity, was a useful asset. Adam Malik was a close friend – often brilliant, liberal in his attitudes, popular with the Angatan '66 – The Generation of '66 – and was known to be bold enough to "stand up to the Bung".

But Ibrahim Adjie was still a problem and, possibly, a danger. His friendship with Sukarno was of long-standing, and he was sore that his leader had been reviled and virtually deposed. Sukarno had helped him when his wife needed medical attention abroad. He was grateful for this and many similar acts of kindness. Suharto knew that Adjie had been summoned to the palace and had, according to reports, undertaken to remain loyal to the President if there should be a showdown. Suharto dared not, at that time, remove him immediately from the command of the Siliwangi Division. He went about it with much more subtlety:

Adjie was given a second-in-command – a Chief of Staff who was eminently trustworthy from Suharto's viewpoint. [Later, in June, he was sent away on a thirteen-week "refresher course" and another general was given his command.]

That front held, Suharto could attend to other things. On March 13 the Sultan of Djogjakarta was summoned to the Palace. Sukarno asked him: "Don't you think that Suharto exceeded the authority given to him when he banned the PKI?"

"How do you mean?" asked the Sultan.

"The Order I gave him covers only technical problems – to use his position as Army commander to bring about a situation of calm in this country. Political decisions are still my prerogative. The decision to ban the PKI was a political one. I have not abdicated my place as President to Suharto. He received his authority from me. There is more authority at the source from which he received his."

The Sultan deflected this approach with great subtlety: "Bung, have you told this to Suharto?"

That ended that conversation. But Sukarno summoned many others and put them through the same catechism. He sent emissaries to Central and East Java and to the commanders of the Navy and the Air Force, making his point that he had not surrendered his power of veto over any decision that Suharto might take as a "technician". The climax of this drive occurred when Chairul Saleh went on television and radio one night to explain to the people "On behalf of the President, Bung Karno, Great Leader of the Revolution, Mandatory of the People's Consultative Congress, Sole Interpretor of the Revolution, etc., etc." that there was much more authority left in the hands of Sukarno and that political decisions were his monopoly.

At Army headquarters, Suharto shrugged his shoulders and commented to his colleagues: "I am not clever at splitting hairs. I was given a job to do and I shall do it. I am expected to bring order to this country and I shall use all means, technical or political, to carry out that task."

The Army commanders, having got over their victory mood, were now becoming apprehensive again about the future. Suharto called a meeting of the High Command and his two closest civilian associates – the Sultan of Djogjakarta and Adam Malik. That afternoon he revealed that he had developed rapidly from "simple soldier – and a good one" to statesman. He told them that he was aware that many of them disapproved of his slow pace, that they wanted to make a "clean break with the past" whatever the cost might be and start "a new order". As he understood the situation, the purpose of his having taken over effective control of power was to "bring Indonesia back to the rule of law – which means the Constitution of 1945." The only meaning of taking power, as far as he was concerned, was to "set precedents for peaceful successions of power in the future." In order to do this there were many problems to overcome, including the resistance of the President against falling into line with new developments. But Sukarno was the lawful President of Indonesia and the Constitution provides for a President. He had been deprived of the excessive powers which he had taken on by decree but he was still the President. Suharto said he would like to see him continue in that position until the succession question was settled by the MPRS – the Consultative Congress which was the source of law in the country. If they did not like his approach and his pace he, Suharto, would willingly step down and allow them to carry on in the way they wished.

There was a stunned, admiring silence. Then, a burst of applause and shouts of "HIDUP PAK 'HARTO".

Suharto's *dukun* had advised that before the next Friday, March 25, he should install the new Cabinet or he would risk losing his own *sakti*. The *guru* had also said that Suharto should reduce the Sukarno Cabinet from "ninety-six to twenty-four, divided into blocks of nine, nine and six." That week was spent in hectic cabinet making.

The first problem was to scrap Sukarno's new Dwikora Cabinet which had created such a storm of public protest. Suharto decided to attack it head on. On March 18 he placed fifteen Cabinet Ministers under "protective custody". They were: Subandrio, Chairul Saleh, Sumardjo (Basic Education), Rekrosoprodjo, Oei Tjoe Tat, Surachman, Jusuf Muda Dalam, Armunanto, Sutomo Martopradota, Astrawinata, Major-General Achmadi, Mohammad Achadi, Colonel Imam Sjafii, J. Tumakaka and Major-General Sumarno.

Along with Achmadi, who had been Minister of Information, his Press Commissar Ganis Harsono who had made platoons of enemies in the world press by playing what the Australian correspondents called "silly buggers" with their copy and their visas, was fired and placed under arrest to be tried for GESTAPU activities.

As soon as the news broke, rumour magnified it. Within hours, the country was buzzing with the story that Subandrio and Chairul Saleh had been executed. A colonel in the Army swore to me that Chief of Police, Sutjipto, had just informed him that he had seen the dead body of Subandrio and was arranging to send his belongings to Mrs Subandrio. Chairul Saleh had been shot at dawn. And, to add piquancy to the tale, my "informant" claimed that he himself had direct knowledge of the fact that General Omar Dani had returned from Pnom Penh at Sukarno's request and had been arrested at Halim air base on his arrival and shot dead immediately. An Army colonel, he said, had been entrusted with the gruesome task of informing Mrs Dani at her house on the Djakarta by-pass that Omar Dani had committed suicide, and of handing her the revolver with which he had been killed.

None of this was true. The information media had become so corrupted during the reign of repression that few took the newspapers or radio seriously, except to pick up bits and pieces to spice the feast of rumour they seemed to relish. The truth was that Subandrio was under "special arrest" in a safe room at the RPKAD barracks off the by-pass. Chairul Saleh was under house arrest. Omar Dani was safely in his Pnom Penh refuge.

President Sukarno himself was now a gilded prisoner. The way this was achieved is an example of the deftness which General Suharto was developing in the handling of men and affairs of State. He disbanded the Tchakrabirawa Regiment, "losing" its personnel in other units which had demonstrated their opposition to the GESTAPU and all it stood for. Then, suddenly, the Presidential helicopter went on the blink. There were no spare parts, it seemed, to repair it sufficiently to guarantee the President's safety. The Army supplied him with one of its own machines with an Army pilot. His instructions were to fly the President between his two palaces in Djakarta and Bogor – and nowhere else. But he was warned that the President must not be made to feel humiliated; every mark of deference must be shown to him. "No pin-pricks" was the rule. So Sukarno flew between his two ornate cages, still enjoying his sybaritic privileges, but no power.

General Suharto and his colleagues continued to pay him the respect due to a President of Indonesia. They bowed low to him, bent down humbly when they had to cross a room in front of him, addressed him as Bapak, and were gentle but firm as though they were dealing with a grandfather who had become irresponsibly senile. On one occasion Sukarno was invited to a meeting with the triumvirate in Djakarta. He arrived in his helicopter but said that he did not feel like working. He complained that he had not been able to see Ratna Devi, his Japanese wife, since her return from America on March 2. Suharto clucked his tongue in concern and invited the President to get into his jeep. Then, with Suharto at the wheel and the Sultan seated behind, the President was given a lift, unescorted by armoured cars or any other fuss, to Devi's house on the outskirts of the city. The General and the Sultan waited outside until the President had finished his business, and drove him back to Merdeka Palace. Perhaps nowhere else in the world would one encounter this kind of delicacy and statesmanship in human relations in such circumstances.

General Suharto warned foreign correspondents who were now being freely admitted that they must try to understand the changes that were taking place and not twist their reports to accommodate their own predilections and prejudices about how things should be. For instance, he said, it would be wrong to refer to what had taken place on March 11 as a "*coup d'état*". It was a lawful succession of power. It would be a mistake to refer to his regime as "a new government". If it *was* a new government, it would have to be recognised anew by all foreign countries. Since this had not happened, it was obviously *not* a new government, he explained in a burst of astonishing logic. Foreign reporters should be careful not to make guesses about Indonesia's new foreign policy or whether he would now release the political prisoners. He was only a soldier and had to study the situation before he could speak about foreign affairs. And, as for the political prisoners, there were only twenty-seven of them – not a bad record compared to other countries – and there was no immediate urgency in dealing with their future. (He was obviously referring to the pre-GESTAPU prisoners, and not to the 200,000 arrested since then.)

General Suharto's tactics were characteristically Javanese. Java is the only country in my experience where "Yes" and "No" may co-exist simultaneously. The Indonesian word that embodies this attitude snugly and expressively is *belum* – and it means "yes, but not yet". Reporters asked him whether he would appoint a new Cabinet. His reply was "*belum*". He was asked whether the Sultan would be announcing a new economic policy. "*Belum.*" Would he stop the *konfrontasi* against Malaysia? "*Belum.*" Would Indonesia rejoin the United Nations? "*Belum.*" Would Indonesia make friends with India? "*Belum.*" Would Indonesia break off diplomatic relations with Peking? "*Belum.*"

It was all very frustrating for diplomats and reporters, but that was the way General Suharto was determined to play it. His major difficulty was what he called *necolimphobie* – the fear of being denounced as a neocolonialist, imperialist puppet. He sensed that even those who had opposed the PKI and the GESTAPU would be squeamish about a sudden *volte face*. His motto therefore was the ancient Javanese saying: *alon alon asal kelakon* – which is another way of saying softly, softly, catchee monkey.

Friday, March 25, the date which his *dukun* had set for the new Cabinet, was fast approaching. Suharto drew up his list of members – putting the Sultan of Djogjakarta as overlord of nine Ministries dealing with economic affairs, Adam Malik as overlord of nine Ministries dealing with political affairs, including foreign relations, and himself in charge of six Ministries concerned with security.

To get Sukarno's formal sanction for this arrangement was the problem. Suharto played a hunch. He telephoned Ratna Devi, the President's fourth wife, and reminded her that she had invited him to *makan* – to have a meal at her house. He said he would like to come that evening together with two friends. She could hardly deny him. That afternoon the Sultan, Adam Malik and Suharto went to *makan*, which included customary Japanese delicacies such as prawn-crackers and jasmine tea. Afterwards Suharto produced his list. He asked Devi if she would help him by taking the list to *Bapak* and telling him that it would be convenient if he would put his signature to it before midnight on Thursday. And his words left no doubt in her mind that if the Bung did not do so, Suharto would have to lean on him a little harder.

On Friday Suharto announced his Cabinet, and having got his team together he set about using it. Sukarno was much more tractable than he had hoped. Once the President made a request: that Suharto should "go easy on Subandrio". Suharto's reply was to this effect: "I have no personal animosity towards 'Bandrio. But what about the people? The people seem to be very angry with him." That was an argument that Sukarno had used so often that he could not reject it now.

The next step was to begin disengaging Indonesia on the Malaysian Front without incurring the criticism of the Afro-Asian bloc and the socialists abroad. For months the Army had been conducting secret negotiations with Kuala Lumpur through Bangkok. There had been a pause on the Malaysian Front since the GESTAPU. Many times during that period Suharto had despatched Lt. Col. Ali Murtopo, a senior intelligence officer of KOSTRAD, to Bangkok and to even Kuala Lumpur to make assessments of the possibilities of a disengagement and an eventual rapprochement. As soon as Suharto took control in Indonesia there were high hopes in Kuala Lumpur and Singapore that confrontation would be called off at once. But it was not so easy when the problem was seen from Djakarta. And, anyway, that was not Suharto's style. He set about it with calculated roundaboutness.

His first overt act concerning *konfrontasi* was to appoint General Nasution as Deputy Supreme Commander of KOGAM, the Crush Malaysia Command that Sukarno had appointed in February. ("Deputy" because Sukarno, of course, was Supreme Commander.) This appointment achieved four preliminary objectives: It brought Nasution out of his black mood and into Suharto's service; the choice of Nasution as head of KOGAM would be read, rightly, in Malaysia as a sign of a thaw; since Nasution was convinced that *konfrontasi* was a political dead-end and an economic disaster for the country, he could be counted upon to liquidate KOGAM and all its ramifications without any heartburn; and finally, it would keep the critics abroad and at home from charging the new regime with selling out to the *necolim.*

The new government settled down to take stock of its problems. The Sultan found that Indonesia's foreign debts now amounted to 2.5 billion dollars. Her few remaining trading partners were not prepared to hold out any longer. Russia was demanding fulfilment of her repayment agreements for the supply of arms and spare parts. Before any foreign trading could be resumed Indonesia needed a cushion of one billion dollars. The food bill was due for settlement and unless it was settled, the people would be deprived of their supplementary rice-supplies – China was no longer willing to fill the Indonesian begging bowl with rice.

The United States and Australia were willing to help, but "*necolim-phobie*" made it necessary not to seem too anxious to make immediate use of this "Western" generosity. Through diplomatic channels Japan was persuaded to propose a meeting of Asian countries willing to help Indonesia. The Japanese Government proposed the formation of a "Tokyo Club" – a consortium of friendly countries willing to provide immediate and long-term assistance to Indonesia.

The Tokyo Club was essentially a multilateral aid scheme which would serve the purpose of making it possible for countries such as the United States and even Britain to come to Indonesia's help without having to go through all the tortuousness of bilateral negotiations. It also made it possible for Indonesia to receive aid from countries with whom she might disagree ideologically. But the Indonesian delegate's brief was, curiously enough, that he should hold out for the continuation of bilateral agreements. This was because the Sultan was being guided by the same bureaucratic experts who had carried out the instructions of Subandrio and Chairul Saleh. Bred on bilaterialism, they found it impossible to see beyond their horizons of suspicion and prejudice. The experience of a country like Ceylon, which had lost itself and the benefits of aid in a maze of bilateral deals with their niggling differences of detail, their varying delivery dates, and the problems they caused in such matters as standardisation of equipment, had obviously not influenced them in the slightest degree.

Not unnaturally, the Sultan was hesitant to change such basic attitudes without more experience and guidance. It soon became clear to him that it would be a grievous mistake to let the bureaucracy dictate his policies and decisions on method, but what could he do? Where were the men he could rely on to advise and guide him through the frightening economic chasm that lay before him? Foreign experts seemed unthinkable for the time being. Like General Suharto he too had to carry out a holding operation, waiting for more propitious opportunities.

Here again Javanese mysticism played its part. According to another hoary prophecy the Sultan of Djogjakarta would "come into his own" soon after mid-1966. Sultan Agung, who had reigned in the ancient kingdom of Mataram (1613–1645), is venerated both for his temporal successes and spiritual sensitiveness. As the opponent of the Dutchman, Jan Pieterzoon Coon, the founder of Djakarta (then Batavia), Sultan Agung was acclaimed a military hero. But he is perhaps even more respected by the Javanese as a man of God and a spiritual seer. On his deathbed Sultan Agung promised that his spirit would "protect the bravest among his descendants" and that forty *windhus* (a windhu is roughly eight years) after his death "all the hopes of his line will be fulfilled".

In 1966, beginning on June 3, the people of Djogjakarta have been commemorating the fortieth *windhu* of the death of Sultan Agung, a fact which has certainly given the Sultan of Djogjakarta heart and direction. The scene of some of the most colourful of these ceremonies was "Imogiri", the mausoleum of Sultan Agung. At the invitation of the Sultan,

General Suharto himself participated in these rituals. For, after all, he and the Sultan are soul-mates.

When the Sultan of Djogjakarta arrived in Bangkok on his way to Tokyo recently, he told the press that the results of the plans now being laid in Djakarta would not materialise until 1970. Was he suggesting this date on the basis of his study of the economic relationships and possibilities available to him in his Ministry files? There is reason to believe that the Sultan is a hard-headed businessman who is not inclined to feel, as Sukarno did, that economics is for book-keepers and not for Ministers of State. But there is also reason to suppose that his certainty about the date is related to another mystical prediction by a spiritual group which has let the Sultan know that 1970 is the date when "Indonesia will experience the beginnings of true peace and prosperity".

Meanwhile Adam Malik was flexing his muscles. Trained as a newspaperman – some say quite a good one – Malik is very different from both Suharto and the Sultan in temperament and character. Malik had served as Ambassador to Russia and had considerable experience elsewhere as a diplomat. He realised, perhaps more than anyone else in the new Cabinet that deep harm had been caused to Indonesia by the paranoiac foreign policies of Sukarno and Subandrio. As soon as Suharto assumed power, Malik is reported to have said that it was time for a "foreign policy revolution". His Cabinet colleagues and his old newspaper friends encouraged him. They wanted to say, in effect, stop the world, I want to get on. The "confrontation" had been costing the country something like sixty per cent of the annual budget. It had certainly also affected Singapore, which had lost about thirty per cent of its business, but the build-up of the British base – from a few battalions to more than 60,000 men – had almost compensated for this loss. The lost business had gone either down the drain or to Hong Kong. From Indonesia's viewpoint it had been an economic disaster. The clandestine contacts made by Ali Murtopo and the messages received through other agencies, such as the exiled socialist party workers, confirmed Malik's assessment that Malaysia and the Philippines were ready to heal the tragic breach without allowing a sense of bitterness to cloud their vision.

Two actions seemed to be indicated; Indonesia should apply to rejoin the United Nations and make open overtures for a settlement of *konfrontasi.* Suharto advised Malik to go slow. The first public indication of events to come was the announcement that Indonesia was considering the formal recognition of Singapore and the resumption of trade. The triumvirate tried it out on the Bung. Malik's approach was to suggest that recognition of Singapore would embarrass and damage Malaysia. That line held. Sukarno gave the scheme his public blessings, but Malik was still uncertain when he could broach the idea of stopping confrontation. Besides the inevitable opposition from the President, there were other major difficulties in the way. There were nearly two divisions of regular soldiers and several thousand "volunteers" on the Sabah-Sarawak border. These men had breakfasted, lunched and dined on the thought of crushing Malaysia for almost three years. How could they be told at once that it was all a big mistake and that Indonesia and Malaysia had really no quarrel at all? If they were brought back to Java they could be a menace.

The Sultan's view at that time was that these men should be kept on in Kalimantan until economic development schemes for Borneo could be started, so that their strength could be diverted to this purpose. His guess was that it would take eight months to a year to get things moving in that direction.

Adam Malik tried another tack. He made a bold announcement that Indonesia would now apply to rejoin the United Nations. This was a trial balloon but it burst right in the Bung's face. In Malik's presence, Sukarno gave an interview to a foreign correspondent during which he brutally contradicted Malik.

It took three months before positive steps could be taken to end the confrontation. Once again the public pressure came from the students' organisations, particularly after Malik disclosed to them how much it was costing the country. The triumvirate decided to confront Sukarno with their plans. The meeting in Bangkok to end confrontation was set up without Sukarno's approval but, as a matter of form, General Suharto, the Sultan, Adam Malik, and General Nasution – in his role as head of KOGAM – called at the Palace.

Sukarno treated them to a long tirade about the genesis and evolution of *konfrontasi* and the dangers of succumbing to the *necolim*. When he had finished, at a nod from Suharto, Adam Malik spoke in a manner that no one in Indonesia had ever before dared to use. It was cold and deliberate. It went something like this: "Bung, your facts are wrong. Therefore your analysis of the situation is wrong. Therefore your policy is wrong. We are determined to go to Bangkok and negotiate the ending of *konfrontasi*."

Sukarno, evidently realising that they had come to tell him what they had decided to do and not to ask his advice, said nothing. The meeting ended on that note.

Within a few days the Bangkok meeting successfully ended the three-year clash between the two Malay neighbours. The public agreement went even further: a proposal was unanimously accepted by Indonesia, Malaysia and Thailand to set up a regional organisation that would be wider and deeper in scope than two previous attempts at cooperation – ASA and MAPHILINDO.

Indonesia agreed to recognise Malaysia. And Malaysia, for her part, agreed to hold general elections "as soon as possible" in Sabah and Sarawak. The letters of agreement do not specify a date but, it appears that there was a "verbal understanding" that it would be in 1967.

This should have satisfied Sukarno's need to save face since it concedes, in principle, his argument that the people of Borneo and Sarawak were not properly consulted before they were absorbed by Malaysia. But he refused to ratify the Bangkok Agreement. Once more there were growls from the younger Army officers who pointed out that if this President would not sign a lawfully negotiated agreement, then they needed a President who would. The students came out in massive demonstrations again demanding the ratification of the peace and, if necessary, the "retooling" of the Presidency. General Suharto again kept a tight hold of the reins. His approach was different. He preferred to wait until the meeting of the People's Consultative Congress which he expected would ratify his policies, including the Bangkok Agreement. The meeting of the Congress ended on July 5. Its decisions were courageous, varied and far-reaching. The 528 representatives attending the Congress resolved, in sum, to put an end to the era of megalomania and set Indonesia on the road to constitutional rule.

They decided:

to strip Sukarno of the right he had assumed to hold the Presidency for life. He would remain President only until the general election, but would retain the title *Pemimpin Besar Revolusi* – Great Leader of the Revolution;

to confirm General Suharto's position as *de facto* executive head;

to hold general elections as soon as possible;

to appoint a "scientific committee" to expurgate the teachings of the Great Leader which they might feel to be contrary to the spirit of the Revolution and the country's real needs;

to hold Sukarno responsible to give the Congress an explanation of the events of September 30 and why his government had failed to develop Indonesia in "the field of economics and public morality";

to revise all decrees and presidential decisions issued since July 1959;

to abolish all honorific titles such as "*Jang Mulia*" (Your Excellency) and use instead the more democratic form of address: *Saudara* (brother);

to ratify the Bangkok Agreement ending *konfrontasi* against Malaysia;

to rejoin the United Nations as an active member;

to ban the propagation and development of the teachings of Communism and Marxist-Leninism;

to annul the grant of the title of *Mahu Putera* (Great Son) which had been granted by Sukarno to D. N. Aidit, the dead communist leader;

to place economic development at the top of the priorities of the country's urgent problems;

to scrap all non-productive efforts and replace them with productive undertakings;

to implement a drastic programme of national austerity;

to reorganise State enterprises, make them more efficient and gear them to increase exports;

to recognise the right to private enterprise in fields which do not 'control' the life of the community as a whole;

and to develop regional institutions so that Indonesia would become a democratic country according to the spirit of the Constitution.

The most significant feature of all this was the firm acceptance – even, perforce, by Sukarno – that the MPRS, the People's Consultative Congress, was the source of all constitutional authority and law.

The defeat of the GESTAPU, the agonising purgation that the populace experienced through six months of murder, and the children's revolution had thus served to end the Sukarno era. Rule by whim has given way to rule by reason and law. Old injustices are being repaired. Sukarno's "private political prisoners", held in jail without trial and at his personal pleasure, have already been released or are to be given a trial. The press has been released from its harshest bonds. Indonesia has already rejoined the International Monetary Fund and will soon rejoin the United Nations.

General Suharto has proved himself to be a man of courage and ability, and seems, so far, to be free of a lust for power for its own sake. He has shown a masterly skill in managing men and in sensing the public mood. But the most valuable quality he has displayed is his ability to wait patiently while everyone round him is fidgeting, and then, when the time seems right, to move fast and decisively. He has revealed an admirable kind of personal detachment which probably comes from his sense of religion and his assessment of himself as an instrument rather than a source of power. His two chief assistants, the Sultan of Djogjakarta and Adam Malik, have the charismatic qualities that give a government the necessary sheen and flavour of popular esteem. And above all, Suharto has the moral weight of constitutional propriety behind him.

But Indonesia's troubles are not over. Its economic and financial problems are terrifying in scope and complexity. Sukarno was the twentieth century Augias and the task of cleaning up the mess of his twenty-year long regime is indeed Herculean. But it would be a mistake to imagine, as many do, that the answer is to divert a massive flow of foreign financial aid through the Indonesian economy. Indonesia abounds in natural recources which, developed, would make it one of the wealthiest countries in the world. But it lacks technical and managerial skills in sufficient depth and quantity for the best intentioned government to be able to make a visible impact for many years. The possibility of internal political upheavals has by no means been eliminated: they have only been swept under a carpet of laws and security precautions. Besides, Sukarno has belied the prognostications of all his doctors and all the political seers and lives on as Head of State. As long as he is alive no one can write him off as a spent force.

POSTSCRIPT

December 31, 1966: Sukarno, who has now been out of effective power for nine months, is still President of Indonesia. Vast crowds still gather to hear him because he is always good theatre, but he has lost the power to mesmerise them into immediate reaction: they even boo and jeer at him. They consider that his time is passed.

His closest associates have been tried for treason and condemned to death by the special tribunal appointed to "get to the bottom of the Gestapu plot" as instructed by the People's Consultative Congress. Yusuf Muda Dalam, Sukarno's Minister of the Central Bank, was found to be his procurer and the source of the misappropriated funds used for political subversion and personal aggrandisement. Dr Subandrio also was convicted of treason as charged. His trial was reminiscent of Eichmann's. His offences were political and his plea was that he was acting according to the policies of the government of the time. But he couldn't convince the court that he had no hand in policy-making. General Omar Dani returned inexplicably from his refuge in Pnom Penh to stand trial. His evidence established that Sukarno at Halim air base on October 1, 1965, had considered going along with the *coup d'état* and knew about the kidnapping of the generals during the night.

But they were only the shadows in the *wayang* puppet drama which the treason trials were. The real struggle was between General Suharto and President Sukarno who never appeared on stage. They say in Djakarta that for Sukarno there is only one of two possibilities: wait out the next assembly of the People's Consultative Congress and face impeachment, or spend the rest of his days abroad as Farouk did. There is a third possibility. Sukarno may still be President when he dies.